D1368454

Karina

E.B. Mann

For Daniel, my Polaris

Speak in French when you can't think of the English for a thing—
Turn your toes out when you walk—
And remember who you are!

— Lewis Carroll, *Through the Looking Glass*

Chapter 1

The cold morning light sliced through the window blinds, illuminating the dust swirling in the center of the room. Karina Morgan lay awake, gazing up at the faded glow-in-the-dark stars her father had affixed to her ceiling all those years ago. The dream she'd been having when the alarm went off sat crouched in the corner of her mind, playing a game of hide-and-seek. She rolled over and hid under the covers, dreading the day that lay before her.

As she dragged herself through her morning ritual —face-washing, tooth-brushing, getting dressed—the weight of what she faced grew heavier. In the kitchen, she crumpled her lunch into her backpack as she fought the urge to run back upstairs and lock herself in the bathroom. Ducking the blows being exchanged between her brothers, she sank into the backseat of her mom's white Honda Pilot with its crushed rear bumper and missing taillight.

The ride to Vista Verde Middle School was, as always, too brief, despite the stop at the elementary school to drop off Max. As the car rattled along, Karina stared out the window, wishing she could ascend to the treetops and leave her empty body behind.

When they pulled up, Jonah threw open the door and ran down the two dozen steps to the low, ivy-covered building. Karina reluctantly followed. The 15-degree drop in temperature upon entering always made her think of an underground tomb. She shivered in anticipation.

On this morning, as she went to open the door—something she'd done a hundred times before—she was stopped in her tracks. The act of reaching for the handle brought her dream screeching back to her. In her mind, she saw a hazy subterranean chamber filled with light. Someone had spoken to her, told her things—important things—though she couldn't remember what. She stood there frozen, staring at the handle in her hand.

"Move it, loser!" growled a voice behind her. She turned to see a 200-pound football player looming over her. She flashed him a sheepish grin, yanked open the door, and went inside.

The air in Mr. Dixon's eighth-grade science class was thick with BO and bad breath, though it was barely 8:30. As she made her way to a desk toward the back of the room, Karina wondered how it could smell so bad so early in the day.

She had long ago developed a habit of sitting near the back of her classrooms—not so far back as to convey disinterest but far enough to provide some cover. She watched as the last of the students trickled in and couldn't help but notice that, despite their gangly bodies and zitty skin, none of them had anything approaching her own hideous imperfection.

Mr. Dixon stood scribbling something on the blackboard. He was a lanky man, old enough to be her grandfather, with a graying goatee, a wild look in his eyes, and a posture that showed the effect of many hours spent bent forward. What he spent those hours bent forward over Karina didn't know, but she liked to picture him hunched before an elaborate laboratory apparatus conducting a groundbreaking experiment that would tear a hole in the fabric of space-time.

Despite his beaten-down appearance, Mr. Dixon was passionate about teaching. In his eyes was a constant low glimmer, like the flame on a Bunsen burner, which would flare up whenever he explained a scientific law or principle. His lighthearted approach to learning made the kids happy to overlook his age and unapologetic nerdiness.

He finished writing, put down the chalk, and turned to face the class, hands clasped in front of his chest as if about to recite a prayer. To the science gods, probably, thought Karina. The class recognized this as a signal he was ready to begin and quieted down.

"Morning, everyone. Okay, um, we were talking about entropy, right?" A handful of students near the front of the room nodded. Mr. Dixon turned to write the word in backward-slanting letters.

With three swishes of his long, spider-like legs, he arrived at his desk in the corner. He grabbed his coffee cup, took a sip, and slammed it down on the desk. The first two rows of students jumped. Karina felt a rush of excitement. She loved Mr. Dixon—he was so theatrical.

"Now, if I had smashed this cup, what would that have been an example of?" Before the class could respond, he held up a finger. "I didn't smash it, of course, because that would have made a huge mess, and I would've had to clean it up. And besides, this is one of my favorite cups. My granddaughter gave it to me for Father's Day. See?" He picked up the cup to show the class the blue-and-gold ribbon painted on the side. "It says 'World's Greatest Grandpa,'" he said, grinning. "So I wouldn't *really* have broken it, but if I *had*, what would that have been an example of?" He returned the cup to the desk as the class murmured the word.

"Yes!" He waved a finger triumphantly in the air and took a step forward. "Entropy: the tendency of everything in the universe, atoms, planets, galaxies—your bedrooms at home…" He paused for an obliging chuckle from the class. "…to disintegrate into a state of disorder. The laws of nature favor entropy. Without a force acting upon things to keep them in a state of order, they will tend toward disorder." He glanced around the room, then returned to his desk.

"This morning, for example, I had a hot cup of coffee. The steam was rising out of it; it smelled great. Brazilian, I think. Premo stuff!" He glanced down into the cup. "I took a sip, but then Principal Sadler came into the room and started talking to me, so I put it down. Eventually, the steam from my coffee dispersed into the air, and the coffee went cold. That is entropy." Mr. Dixon looked intently at the class.

"The heat from my coffee spread out into the room and was no longer organized inside the cup. The temperature of the coffee and the temperature of the room reached *equilibrium*." He turned to write the word on the blackboard. "So, has the heat disappeared?" A few students shook their heads. "That's right. Energy—in this case heat—cannot be destroyed. That is what is known as the *conservation* of energy. The energy is no longer organized inside the cup, but it still exists… somewhere… out there." Mr. Dixon fluttered his hands and widened his eyes spookily.

Karina picked up her pen to write "conservation of energy" in her notebook, but her attention was immediately drawn to the doodles she'd made the previous week when Mr. Dixon had been sick and they'd had a sub. There were the usual schoolgirl squiggles: a cloud with a rainbow jutting out of it, a vase full of flowers, and a heart containing the name of her fondest obsession: Parker Anderson.

Seeing the name of the roguishly handsome Parker, who was the object of desire for so many girls at Vista Verde, conjured up his face, and despite Karina's interest in the lesson, she lost her focus. Though she continued to stare at Mr. Dixon, her eyes glazed over, and she was swallowed by the memory of the first time she'd laid eyes on the magnificent boy who'd occupied her every waking moment for months. As she'd done so many times before, Karina recalled the exact moment her heart had shattered into a million pieces, each tiny fragment stamped with his initials.

It had been late October. Karina had been leaning against a wall waiting for Jonah's soccer practice to end when she'd noticed Parker on the sidelines. His mother had been talking to him while he sat taking off his cleats, and he'd been ignoring her. After a few attempts to get him to respond, she'd given up and reached down to tousle his hair. When he'd turned to swat her away, Karina had caught sight of his bronzed cheeks, smoky brown eyes, and wicked sideways smile. One flick of that dirty blonde hair, and her fate had been sealed.

From that moment on, Karina had known that if ever there might lurk in the darkest recesses of her heart—in the places reserved for the most delicate of feelings—a single desolate hope for romantic happiness, it would forever dangle from those luscious, shiny locks.

On that day, to her parents' surprise, Karina developed a sudden interest in her brother's soccer career. She'd sit on the sidelines and cheer, hoping—and yet fearing—that Parker would notice her. Although it was obvious that this boy was miles beyond her reach, that he rated someone at the very top of the Vista Verde social scale, and despite her best efforts to reason with herself, Karina couldn't help but yearn for him. She was smitten—hopelessly, recklessly, unconditionally smitten.

She was sitting there enjoying the buzz of pleasant feelings flowing through her body, when her daydream suddenly splintered and a stinging memory rose up to take its place.

A few weeks after she'd first noticed him, Karina had run into Parker on his way to the parking lot.

Mistaking his brief glance in her direction for a sign of recognition, she'd been overtaken by an uncharacteristically bold impulse. Before she could stop herself, her mouth had begun to form words—something that had startled even her.

"Are you going to Borelli's after the game, Parker?" He'd paused to look at her, his contorted grimace registering a mix of surprise and irritation.

"What's it to you, freak?" he'd said, his words like bullets ripping through her flesh. In an instant, she'd been gripped by nausea, almost as if she'd actually been shot. Her head had begun to spin and every muscle to give out. She'd staggered and caught herself just before face-planting onto the pavement. All of this had occurred with barely an outward sign. But to Karina, on that day, it'd felt as if she'd almost lost her life.

"Parker, that's not nice!" his mother had said, smiling at her through the car window. "Sure, we'll be there." When her eyes had come to rest on Karina's face, though, her smile had faded.

From the curb, Karina had watched the car pull away, Parker in the passenger's seat, a pair of earphones jammed into his ears, completely unaware of the brutal homicide he'd almost committed.

Chapter 2

Karina squeezed her petite frame through the crush of students and arrived at her locker, decorated with a SpongeBob magnet, a heady quote from the Dalai Lama, and a peace-sign bumper sticker. She quickly entered her combination, and using the door as a shield, began to unload her backpack.

On the inside of the door was a small mirror which was nearly obscured by the blue and white silk flowers she'd taped around it. As was her habit, she paused to check her reflection.

She was not technically ugly: round, pink cheeks; small, dimpled chin; wavy, golden hair. When her eyes, hidden as they were under heavy bangs, did meet those of another, their soft green hue and intelligent gleam were generally deemed attractive.

She swiped at an imaginary smudge on her chin and then, with slight hesitation, brushed aside her bangs to reveal the reason she was so thoroughly despised, the small but horrible reason no one would ever be able to call her pretty. From the right-hand corner of her forehead to the spot where her left eyebrow began, carving a torturous path and buckling the skin as it went, was an agonizing, impossible-not-to-notice, simply vicious three-inch scar.

The deep gash stared out at the world and was the first thing most people noticed about her. A ghastly emissary shouting "look away!", it repelled every man, woman, and child she encountered before they ever had the chance to notice the girl beneath.

She gazed sadly at her reflection as she struggled to train her hair flat against her forehead, then closed her locker, picked up her backpack, and headed to class.

"Karina!" She could hear Mary Blair's voice above the din of students chatting and banging their locker doors. She turned to see a mass of dreadlocked, brownish purple hair bouncing toward her through the crowded hallway. Her friend's sarcastic grin was one of the few things she liked about being at school. "Karina!" she called, out of breath.

"Hey," said Karina. "What happened? D'you get busted?" Mary Blair's freckled cheeks were flushed from running and her forehead glistened. Her baggy, menswear corduroys and quirky multicolored scarf clashed with her black horn-rimmed glasses. Tangled locks poked out from beneath the fuzzy pom-pom beret she'd knitted herself.

"What do *you* think? It took me 45 minutes to get home. Also, I got a D on my algebra quiz, so…," she shrugged. They turned the corner and started down the school's main hallway. "I think I'm gonna ditch PE today. My mom wrote me a note 'cause I got a visit from my Cousin Tom." She hitched her overstuffed backpack onto her shoulder.

"Who?"

"You know," she whispered. "Time of the month."

"So you're all KFC then?" asked Karina. "Kinda feeling crampy?"

"Totally," said Mary Blair, smirking and clutching her stomach. "Anyway, Marco's picking me up after school. We're gonna hang at the pier. You should come." Karina suspected Mary Blair was doing it with Marco, the creepy high-school boyfriend she'd met trying to buy beer outside the 7-11. He was bad news. She tried to smile.

"Got a lot of homework," she said. Mary Blair shot her a disapproving look.

"Alright. See ya later."

"See ya," said Karina. "And be careful, dude."

"I never am!" Mary Blair shouted over her shoulder as she turned the corner.

Karina shook her head and continued down the

hallway. She was glad Mary Blair had decided to become her friend, despite her wild ways. If not for her, Karina would have literally zero friends at Vista Verde. Her association with Mary Blair had placed her solidly in the "rebel" category, which was a step up from "desperate loser." More importantly, she thought as she exited the main building on her way down to English, Mary Blair saw past her scar to the person she was on the inside, the girl she would've been if only she hadn't tripped on that goddamn crack.

A woman of about fifty, Mrs. Swanson was in the habit of propping open the door to her poorly ventilated mobile classroom. She sat grading papers at her desk, growing increasingly annoyed by the noise coming from the basketball courts outside. When the sound of the ball bouncing on the blacktop became unbearable, she got up, muffin top hanging sloppily over her skirt, and went to go shut it.

Before she reached the door, a couple of girls strode in laughing. When they saw the frown peeking out from beneath her helmet of mousy-brown hair, they quickly took their seats.

"Okay, everyone, I'm still working on your papers. I should have them back by tomorrow. So today we're going to do a free-writing exercise," she said, pointing to the blackboard where she'd written "Defining Personal Experience." "The topic is an experience you've had that's had a major impact on your life—good or bad. Something that's helped shape who you are today." The students got out their pens and notebooks. Karina sighed and opened hers. There was really only one thing that qualified. She wrote "My Scar" at the top of the page and stared at it. She had no idea where to begin.

She'd been little more than two when, one otherwise perfectly fine day, her shoe had gotten caught on the backyard pavement outside her childhood home. So bad was the ensuing tumble that it had become family lore, an episode she knew only from tales her mother told of that "awful day" she was "almost blinded."

And although it had had an enormous effect on the person she'd become and had come to define her in the minds of so many, the memory of her fall was lost, sealed off in an infancy beyond her recollection.

There weren't even any photographs of her from that time that might've helped her remember. Because of this—though she'd worn the gruesome reminder of it every day since—it always seemed as if her fall had happened to someone else. She shook her head, crossed out the title, and wrote "My Trip to Disneyland."

After climbing the steps back to the main building,

Karina entered through the side door. She began to feel sick to her stomach, just as she always did in this part of the school. By the time she'd rounded the corner on her way to her next class, her throat had completely closed and she was struggling to breathe. She pressed her eyes shut, jammed her chin against her chest, and aimed for the classroom at the end of the hall.

She'd gotten only a third of the way there, though, when her path was blocked by a row of long, shapely legs in expensive designer heels. She recoiled at the sight of five stunningly beautiful girls curling their lips at her as if she were a steaming puddle of vomit. Karina beheld The Beautiful Bitches.

"There she is," said Emma, a tall blonde with impossibly long eyelashes and a small, turned-up nose. "Gross!" she laughed. Karina had heard rumors that Emma had worked as a model over the summer and had even gotten an agent. But Emma—a formidable foe in her own right—was still only second in command. The supreme position was held jointly by the black-haired, brilliantly blue-eyed devils and identical twins Amanda and Avery.

Their lean, catlike bodies were slinky vessels of pure evil, their eyes gleaming with frosty pleasure at the torture they inflicted on their prey. A redhead and another blonde, masters at the art of whispered contempt, rounded out The BB ranks.

"Hey, Scarina, I have something that might help your, um, condition," said Avery, reaching inside her locker and pulling out a clump of wet clay she'd stolen from the ceramics studio. She held it up, sneered cruelly, and heaved it at Karina. It came up short, landing at her feet and splattering wet chunks all over her shoes.

Though Karina's eyes began to water, she clamped down, determined not to cry in front of The Bs and the small crowd that had gathered to watch. It was all she could do to push past them and run down the hall, mocking laughter echoing in her ears.

Chapter 3

Legend of Zelda, the year's hottest gaming obsession, had Karina's brothers and every other boy (and some girls) firmly in its clutches. As she trudged upstairs, she could hear the shouts and groans coming from her brothers' darkened bedroom. Karina had learned that while in the midst of a game, a blow to the back of the head would almost not be enough to distract them from the screen.

Jonah, older than his brother by almost two years but only slightly taller due to a thyroid condition that had stunted his growth, had been mortally wounded.

"Scrote-face!" he shouted, tossing aside his controller and lunging at Max. He was poised to attack, when they heard the grinding of the garage door that signaled their father's return home.

"Dad's here, guys!" Karina's mom yelled up the stairs. "Dinner!"

At the little desk in her room, Karina tucked her completed history homework into her backpack. She checked her day planner for the next day's assignments, scribbling a reminder to stop by the library on her way home from school. She paused to survey her tidy little room, nodding her approval before closing the door.

The contrast between the order and discipline Karina had created for herself and the chaos swirling through the rest of the house was jarring. She'd barely taken two steps into the hallway, strewn with backpacks, toys, and dirty socks, when the boys came running at full speed toward her, screaming and violently thumping each other. Despite her best evasive maneuvers, Karina was thrown back against the wall.

They tussled their way to the end of the hall, where Max, chubby cheeks flushed with heat, was losing the battle. He lunged forward and attempted to punch Jonah in the crotch before retreating down the stairs. Jonah dodged the blow and delivered a roundhouse kick to the kidneys, losing his glasses in the process.

Max went tumbling headfirst down the stairs and, after an awkward partial somersault during which he banged his head against the wall, caught the handrail and skidded to a halt. He turned to glare up at Jonah before collapsing in a heap of tears.

"Mom, Jonah pushed me down the stairs!" Max shrieked through his sobs.

"Jonah! Stop that right now!" their mother yelled from the kitchen. As Jonah skipped passed him, Max, who was continuing his lament, reared back and swung his fist so wildly that he was sent toppling the rest of the way down the stairs.

"Dick-spank!" screamed Max when he landed at the bottom. Jonah calmly returned his glasses to his nose, gave him a devilish smirk, and escaped into the kitchen.

Karina stood patiently at the top of the stairs waiting for the wild animals with whom she shared a home to conclude their death match. Most days, it was all she could do to avoid getting between them. When they were really after each other, which was most of the time—slapping, kicking, pounding, biting, snatching each other's things, chasing each other around, wrestling, poking, screaming, crying, knocking each other down, farting in each other's faces—she would simply retreat to her neatly kept sanctuary and lock the door.

"Hi, baby," Karina's dad said, dragging himself through the front door. She approached and wrapped her arms around his belly, pressing her cheek against his stained tie. "How was your day?"

"Okay," said Karina, dredging up a cheerful tone. As she followed him into the kitchen, she couldn't help but notice how sandy his once-dark hair had become. Karina's mom poked her head out from the kitchen, forehead glistening with sweat.

"Hi, honey. How'd it go?" she asked.

"Same crap, different day," he said, lugging his briefcase into the small office/storage room beyond the kitchen. Karina approached the table, where her brothers stood arguing.

"That's my cup, cock-jockey!" said Max, snatching a plastic Spiderman tumbler out of Jonah's hand. Jonah shrugged and picked up another cup. Still fuming, Max yanked his chair out from under the table, accidentally crushing Jonah's toe.

"That's my toe, dingle-breath!" Jonah's eyes glowed with anger, while his father flashed him a disapproving look.

"I didn't mean to," said Max, but Jonah punched him in the bicep anyway.

"Ow!" squealed Max.

"Everyone! Please!" said Karina's mom, palms turned upward, fingers curled in pleading desperation. It was a pose they all recognized as a sign she was nearing her breaking point. The boys blanched at the prospect of another one of her infrequent but terrifying meltdowns and took their seats. Karina and her dad did the same.

Karina's mom took a deep breath and began

ferrying the plates to the table. Pork chops were not her specialty. Somehow they always seemed to get away from her and end up resembling chunks of broken asphalt. Karina stared at the dismal plate before her: mushy gray-green beans; dry, barely mashed potatoes; and a three-inch piece of shriveled corn on the cob.

"Sorry about the burned parts, guys," she said, placing a conciliatory bottle of ketchup on the table. The words seemed to exhaust the last of her energy.

"It's fine, hon. Sit down," said Karina's dad. She ignored him and returned to the kitchen to grab a pitcher of ice water. He glanced at Karina's plate. "No pork chop tonight, honey?" he asked and then whispered, "I don't blame you."

"I'm a vegetarian, Dad," she said, annoyed at having to remind him.

"Oh, yeah. I forgot," he said, picking up his fork. Karina rolled her eyes.

"So, how was the meeting?" Karina's mom asked her husband, finally collapsing into her chair.

"We spent the entire two and a half hours on Y2K. My presentation got postponed—again," he said. He was just about to deposit a forkful of mashed potatoes into his mouth when the phone rang.

"Probably another one of those pain-in-the-ass

telemarketers," he said, reaching for the phone on the counter behind him. "Hello?" he shouted into the receiver, but after a few seconds, it was clear this wasn't a sales pitch. "Oh, hi. How are you doing?" he said, suddenly respectful. He mouthed the word "Gram" to his wife and stood up. "Oh, good! Oh, no, we were just sitting down to dinner. Absolutely. Uh-huh," he said, glancing at Karina. "Yeah, sure, she's right here." He handed her the phone. Karina swallowed quickly and took it into the living room.

"Hello?" she said.

"Darling?" said Gram.

"Hi, Grammy!"

"Hi, Sweetpea. How are you?"

"Good."

"Hey, I was going to come for lunch this Sunday, but I wanted to make sure my favorite granddaughter'll be there." Karina could hear the smile on her face.

"Gram, I'm your only granddaughter."

"I know…," she said laughing, "…but you're still my favorite."

"Sure, yeah, that sounds great," said Karina.

"Good. I miss you so much!" said Grammy.

"I know. Me too."

"How's school? Everyone being nice to you?"

"Yeah, you know, the usual." Karina shrugged.

"Well, Karina, you just remember that I think you hung the moon, okay?"

"Okay."

"I have a surprise for you."

"What is it?" asked Karina.

"I guess you'll just have to wait and see."

"Awww!"

"Ha, ha, ha, hee!" Grammy was clearly enjoying the tease. "Gotta go, honey. See you Sunday."

"Okay, 'bye!" Karina hung up and returned to her place at the table.

"Gram says she's going to come on Sunday," she said in response to her mother's inquiring look.

"Oh, yeah, I forgot," said Karina's mom, turning to her husband. "We're going to do some shopping and then get lunch." The boys looked crestfallen.

"Do we have to go?" asked Max.

"Yes, you have to go," said their father. The boys pouted into their plates.

"She's got a present for me!" said Karina, smiling. The boys shot her a jealous look.

"Really?" said Karina's mom, looking surprised. "I wonder what it is."

"That's not fair! Why does Karina get a present? It's not her birthday!" whined Jonah.

"Yeah! It's not her birthday," echoed Max.

"Boys, try to be grateful for all the things you do have, okay?" said Karina's dad. "Besides, it's probably something girlie."

"But…," Jonah protested.

"Who wants ice cream?" interrupted Karina's mom, jumping up to grab a carton out of the freezer.

"Me! Me!" said the boys.

The miseries of the day finally losing their edge, Karina decided to take her father's advice and count her blessings: a bowl of chocolate ice cream and a visit—and a present!—from Gram.

Chapter 4

After dinner, Karina's parents went upstairs to get ready for bed, while Karina and Jonah sat on the couch watching *The Simpsons*. Max was lying on the floor petting Henry, the Morgans' terrier. The show ended, and Jonah started bragging about the cheat he'd found in the seventh level of Zelda. When Max didn't respond, Jonah stuck out his leg and whacked him on the back of the head with his shoe.

"Ow! What'd ya do that for?" asked Max, turning to glare at him and rubbing his head. Jonah let out a joyless chuckle and took off running.

"I get the good chair," he said, already halfway up the stairs.

"No, you don't!" said Max, springing to his feet. Karina grabbed him by the back of the shirt.

"Why are you guys always fighting?" she asked.

"I don't know." He shrugged. "I try to be nice to him, but he's always such an anus. He just hates me, I guess," he said, turning to trudge upstairs.

Karina picked up the remote and began flipping through the channels, stopping on an old 1970s documentary.

"...*parapsychologist Satwant Pasricha of the National Institute of Mental Health in Bangalore. One of Dr. Pasricha's best-documented cases was that of Manju, who at the age of two claimed to recall life as another little girl who'd drowned in a well. Manju, a married woman with two daughters of her own, lives in the Hindu holy city of Brindaban in Northern India. The drowning occurred in a nearby village.*

An Indian woman wearing a sari and standing under a tree appeared on the screen and began to speak.

"*I remembered drowning in a well when I was ten. This was in Chumha village. When I was two-and-a-half years old, I happened to see my uncle from before. I told him who I was, but he said, 'Our child drowned in a well.' I told him again that he was my uncle, so he brought me to my mother. She seemed to recognize me and put me on her knee and gave me sweets.*"

The narrator resumed speaking.

"*Manju's feelings were so strong that as a child she insisted on living with the drowned girl's family. Now that she is an adult, Manju no longer fears wells, not even the well where she believes she once drowned.*"

The screen switched to another Indian lady, this one dressed in a lab coat and seated behind a desk.

"I would consider this a very strong case. She began to talk about her previous life at a very young age— only two-and-a-half—and when she would talk about her memories, her facial expressions would change, as if she were feeling genuine emotions. I didn't believe that at that age, she could be coached to make such claims."

Karina watched the rest of the show, which included the stories of two other children, and found the scientists' attempts to verify their recollections utterly convincing. She turned off the TV and stared at the darkened screen. Well, that's it, she thought, reincarnation really is real.

Henry, who had been watching her, started to whine, so she stood up.

"C'mon, Henry, let's go see if there're any creatures out tonight." Henry followed her to the sliding glass door leading out to the backyard. She opened it, and Henry bounded out, barking fiercely. He headed to the far corner of the yard, where the grass met some bushes, and jammed his nose into a tiny hole. He was panting and barking and frantically trying to dig out the hole.

"What's in there, Henry, huh?" asked Karina, approaching. She bent down to stroke his back, but he ignored her and continued to dig, so she gave up. Ambling toward the center of the lawn, where the grass was dense and green, she threw back her head to take in the sky, awash in blue and violet. She began to count the stars just coming into view: one, two, three, four.

When Henry let out a frustrated squeal, she went back over to him. He looked pleadingly at her, then back at the hole.

"Whatcha got, buddy?" she asked. Though he was determined to get at whatever was in there, to Karina it just looked like an empty hole. "You're crazy, dog!" she said, snatching him up in her arms.

She was staring down at the hole, when something on the other side of the fence caught her eye. In the corner of the yard next door, the neighbor boy, who Karina barely ever spoke to, was sitting on a weathered rattan chair. His jeans were torn and his hair looked like it hadn't been washed in a week. His dirty bare feet were resting on a wooden cable spool he was using as a table.

Click, click. Through the bushes Karina watched as the boy repeatedly flicked a cigarette lighter a few inches from his face. The evening breeze wafted the smell of smoke in her direction. Apparently unaware that he was being watched, the boy took puff after puff on a small metal pipe.

As she stood there cuddling Henry against her shoulder and stroking his back, Karina wondered what was wrong with this boy that he was always alone. He never had friends over and had refused her brothers' early invitations to play. They barely ever saw his wheelchair-bound mother. In fact, it was a joke at their house that he'd killed her and was living off her disability checks. He didn't appear to have a father.

When Henry, who was still fascinated by the hole, started to bark and squirm in her arms, Karina carried him away from the fence, afraid that the boy would hear and realize she'd been watching him. To calm him, Karina began singing softly into his ear.

"Silly dog. Barky-bark. You're a silly doggy." It seemed to work because he stopped barking and looked up at her. She smiled and kissed his snout. As she stroked his head and gazed into his eyes, Karina thought she saw as much awareness, as much "soul" there as in any human being's—more so, in the case of some people she knew.

She tucked his head under her chin and wandered toward the back of the Morgans' property line. Here the lush grass and manicured hedge gave way to a wooded area with a trail that sloped down to a rocky creek. Karina put Henry down, and he scampered off, disappearing down the trail.

Karina followed, relieved to be out of the house and away from her brothers' constant fighting and her parents' tense exhaustion. She wondered why nobody in her family ever seemed happy. Sure, there were happy moments, like the time her dad had gotten the job at the factory. That had been a good day. She'd come home from school to a frenzied scene—her father hurling her mother in a circle in the middle of the living room. Her dad had performed a totally embarrassing dance, while her mother had laughed and clapped. There had been a lot of hugging and some grateful tears. Her parents had seemed so young that day, so alive.

That evening, they'd enjoyed a wonderful meal at the fancy steakhouse near the fountain at the center of town, the one where Vista Verde families went to celebrate special occasions.

Yes, she thought, there were times like those, times that brought a smile to her face. But her father's job had come only after a grueling, 18-month search that had nearly killed him. He'd slipped into a depression, started drinking too much, and ended up in the ICU with a stomach ulcer. Once he was stable, the family had gone to visit him. Lying in his hospital bed, deathly pale with all those tubes sticking out of him, he'd been almost unrecognizable. Max had stood by his bed, crying and repeatedly asking "Where's Daddy?" It had been the longest three days of Karina's young life.

That night, at home, Karina had stood in the kitchen and watched her mother cry. It was one of only two times she'd ever seen her mother cry, the other being after Grampa's fatal heart attack. The sight of her mother standing at the sink dripping tears onto the dirty dishes had scared the crap right out of her.

Everyone was so grateful when her dad made a quick recovery and returned home a few days later. When he was finally offered the job, Karina knew her parents' happiness was actually mostly relief. They wouldn't have to pile into Gram's spare bedroom after all.

Now, three years later, the daily dose of abuse from his incompetent boss, the crushing boredom of the same thing day after day, the political backstabbing and sabotage by subordinates, the physical toll of eight hours spent crouched at a tiny desk, and the insultingly low pay had long ago eclipsed any happiness he'd felt at landing the job at N-lighten Home Lighting Solutions.

Karina looked up from her reverie and realized that she'd reached the spot where the trail dissolved onto the sandy banks of the creek. She stopped to listen to its gentle gurgle and heard the rustle of a night creature on the opposite bank.

Remembering Henry, she glanced around and called his name. When she got no response, she called back up the trail, thinking perhaps he'd returned home.

"Henry! Where are you?"

Suddenly, she heard a panicked barking coming from somewhere downstream. She scrambled down the rocky bank and paused to listen. Henry's pathetic whimper was coming from beyond an embankment where the creek took a turn.

"Henry? Henry? Are you okay?" she called out as she clambered awkwardly around the embankment. Henry's barking had reached a desperate pitch, when Karina spied his tail protruding from a clump of branches growing against the bank. She let out a sigh of relief when she saw that it was wagging.

"There you are! What are you...?" Karina scooped him up and was turning to head back toward the trail, when she noticed something near the spot where he'd been rooting around. In the light of the rising moon, something shiny glinted among the branches. She paused to see what it could be, but the thick overhang of foliage was blocking her view. She glanced down at Henry, who was watching her expectantly.

Stepping closer, she craned her neck to get a better look. Yes, there was definitely something in there. She set

Henry down and began clearing away the branches. When she encountered a particularly thick one, she leaned on it with all her weight until it snapped, revealing a giant cobweb. She grimaced and tore it away, then went back to removing the leaves and branches.

Once she could see the object clearly, she stood there stunned, hardly able to believe her eyes. There, shining dully in the darkness, was an old-fashioned, brass door handle!

"What the…?" She reached her hand between the remaining branches, and the tips of her fingers brushed against cold metal. She let out a little gasp and withdrew her hand.

"What *is* that?" she asked, turning to Henry, but he'd lost interest and was sniffing the dirt a few feet away.

The creek bed dark and eerie in the twilight, Karina felt a lump rise in her throat. She knew her parents would soon be wondering where she was. Still, she just had to investigate this mystery. Who would mount a brass door handle into a dirt embankment?

She stood there for a moment, struggling to make sense of it.

Chapter 5

The day was aging quickly, each minute darker than the last. Karina placed her foot on a large root growing along the ground and again stretched out her hand. With just a whisper between the tips of her fingers and the handle, she reached as far as she could, lost her balance, and fell forward. This time, her fingers brushed against the slats of an old wooden door. She turned to gape at Henry, who had returned to her side.

"It's a door!" she said. Henry barked in agreement. After a playful twirl, he clamped down on a branch and began gamely tugging at it.

As she stood there watching him, Karina felt a strange sensation come over her, as if she'd begun to pull away from herself and was watching the scene unfold from somewhere overhead. The embankment, the creek, and Henry took on a dreamy, faraway quality. The impossibility of her discovery—an improbable door in an improbable place—made her head swirl.

She was starting to think she might faint, when Henry let out a loud, insistent yelp, and she was jolted back to her surroundings. When she saw him frantically tugging at the branches, she snapped into action.

Together they removed the remaining leaves and branches until the door was completely uncovered. Karina stopped to catch her breath. The door was caked in dust and looked as if it could be a hundred years old. The richly weathered wood told the story of many years of exposure to the elements, and the handle was speckled with rust. The door and its frame, at only four and a half feet tall, reminded her of the old European houses she'd seen in movies. Could someone be living in there? she wondered.

She stepped forward and blew on the handle. A cloud of dust billowed into the air. She waved it away, then carefully ran her hand along the wood grain. The texture was rough, and the handle looked as if it might fall off.

Unsure what to do next, Karina backed away, glancing upstream to see if she could see anyone in the gloom. She held her breath, half-expecting Mary Blair, her brothers—anyone—to jump out from behind a bush and tell her she'd been punk'd. But except for the water trickling quietly over the rocks, the creek bed was silent.

For a moment, she stood there debating whether to run back to the house to tell her parents what she'd found but knew they'd only laugh at her.

"Why would anyone build a door in the side of a hill?" Karina whispered to herself. And how was it that no one else had ever discovered it before now? Sure, it'd been hidden by overgrowth, but she'd spotted it relatively easily. And this begged another question: How was it that she'd never seen it before? She'd walked along this creek a million times and had never noticed it. It made absolutely no sense. She found herself shaking her head, as if to deny the reality of what she was seeing.

With the hour late and Karina barely able to see her hand in front of her face, she resolved to make her move—whatever that might be. She looked again at Henry, who was panting and wagging his tail.

"Okay, okay," she said, thrusting back her shoulders. She stepped toward the door, grabbed the handle and turned it. When it wouldn't budge, she felt a rush of relief mixed with disappointment. She jiggled it a few times, then froze when she heard the latch click. Her heart pounded in her ears as she tugged on the handle, only to discover that the door was stuck in the jamb. She summoned her strength, grabbed the handle with both hands, and pulled on the door until it finally creaked open. A puff of stale air hit her in the face.

She coughed and covered her mouth, then peered

around the door to see a dark passageway stretching out before her. When her eyes, wide with fear and wonder, had adjusted to the darkness, she was able to make out the walls and ceiling of the tunnel and noticed that the floor was covered in dark, moist earth. The smell of rotting vegetation tickled her nose. She leaned forward, squinting, but could see only a few feet inside. She thought she could make out a bend at the end of the tunnel, beyond which she couldn't see.

Resisting the urge to bolt back to the trail, back to her house, back to anywhere but here, she set her jaw in determination. She knew what she was about to do was in no way sensible, but something propelled her forward.

The sound of the rusty hinges as she opened the door the rest of the way sent a strange echo down the tunnel, and Karina got the impression that it'd been a very long time since anyone had been inside. Henry whined nervously and stepped back, shaking his head.

"It's okay," she told him, though her tone was uncertain. "We'll go in together." She bent down to pat his head, then stood to face the tunnel. She ducked through the doorway and planted a foot in the soft dirt. The air was thick and heavy. She stilled herself for a moment to listen and thought she could hear a faint whoosh of air circulating at the far end of the tunnel.

Still fighting the urge to retreat, Karina took two more hesitant steps into the musty darkness, her shoe squishing into a mud puddle. She turned around to look for Henry, who was standing resolutely beyond the door.

"Come on, Henry," she said. Though he was barely ten pounds, Karina knew she'd feel safer with him by her side. Henry took a few steps backward and barked his refusal. "Go home, then!" she said with a flash of anger. He hesitated, let out one last disapproving yelp, and ran off in the direction of the house. Karina turned back to peer down the tunnel. She held her breath for a moment.

"What the hell," she said offhandedly and began to feel her way along. A few yards in, the passageway began to descend. She rounded the bend in complete darkness, then saw a faint glow coming from the other end. For a moment, she thought the light must mean that the tunnel led back outside but then remembered the sun had already set. It couldn't be daylight. As she drew closer, her mind struggled to understand where the light could be coming from. Trembling, she began to wonder if she ought to have followed Henry home.

Not knowing whether to trust her own eyes, Karina made her way along until the tunnel widened into a large open area, a room of sorts, filled with light. As she approached the opening, the tunnel floor seemed to change. Gone was the soft, damp earth, as her shoes encountered something hard and crunchy. She glanced down and was dumbfounded to see ice beneath her feet—in a region where it never snowed!

She crunched her way down the last few feet of the tunnel and emerged into a large cavern. She stepped forward tentatively, stopping to allow her eyes to adjust to the bright shimmer of the place. Through the mist of her now-visible breath, a huge cave made entirely of ice came into view. It was a sight so unbelievable Karina could only stand there and stare. Though a shiver ran through her, to her amazement, she realized she didn't feel cold.

The soaring ceiling dripped with icicles, and dangling from the longest were ornate chandeliers chiseled from tinkling chunks of ice. The candlelight glinting off the icicles made the walls and ceiling appear to dance with shadows. And though the candles in these chandeliers flickered with flame, the ice did not appear to be melting.

Along the walls, which resembled sheared-off icebergs, were soaring stained glass windows like the ones she'd seen in church. Instead of Bible scenes, though, these windows displayed iridescent, fractal designs of a hypnotic, three-dimensional nature.

On the floor of the cave was a snowy lawn dotted with rocks, trees, and bushes—all made of ice. Encircling it all was a frozen stream. Karina spotted a couple of pieces of wooden furniture, but the general appearance of the place was a cross between an ancient cathedral and an arctic garden. The ceiling, carved from giant blocks of ice, sloped up toward a kind of altar at the back of the cave. Here the light was so bright and clear, it made Karina's eyes water. It was the prettiest place she'd ever seen.

Directly in front of her, a small wooden bridge crossed the stream. She took a step toward it, and her shoe caught on a tangle of clear vines. When she bent down to free it, she was struck by the vines' composition. Each tiny, translucent leaf was perfect down to the last detail.

She stepped onto the bridge and glanced over the edge at the frozen stream, then continued across and approached an ice tree in the center of the lawn. The flickering candlelight made it appear to sway. On one of its glittering branches, an ice bird sat perched with its beak open, as if flash frozen in mid-tweet. Each tiny tail feather distinct from the others, it appeared utterly lifelike, as if it might break into song at any moment. Karina shook her head in disbelief and again surveyed the cave.

"There is simply no way that this is…" she said, gazing up at the extraordinary spectacle. As she stood there taking it all in—the grass, the trees, the stream—it struck her as a strange mockery of nature. What should have been alive and thriving was frozen solid. An ice cave hidden underground—it was a beautiful mystery that defied explanation. She decided she simply had to tell her parents what she had found and was turning to leave, when she heard a man's voice echo through the cave.

"Good evening, young lady."

Karina choked back a scream. She spun around and peered toward the altar. Through the intense glow emanating from the back of the cave, the seated figure of a man came into view. She was both embarrassed at having trespassed into his space and startled by the sudden realization that she was not alone.

"Who are…?" She glanced around nervously, wondering who else might be lurking in this icy wonderland. "What are you doing here?" Karina stepped forward to get a better look at him.

"Yes," he laughed. "That is the question exactly: What am I doing here? What are any of us doing here?"

He stood up from his seat behind the altar. The light pouring from the towering window behind him made it difficult to see anything but a dark silhouette. She shaded her eyes and was able to make out the imposing figure of a man of about 60 with bushy white eyebrows and a white beard trailing down his chest. His white hair was pulled back into a messy ponytail and tucked under a round, white hat, and his white fur coat swept the floor. Despite his rather scraggly appearance, there was something distinctly regal about him.

As the man stepped out from behind the altar, the vertigo Karina had experienced outside the cave suddenly returned. She shifted on her feet, and for a moment, doubted her ability to stay upright. She took a deep breath and ordered herself to get a grip. Although nothing seemed to be making much sense, she was determined to assess her situation: Here, in an ice cave, in the side of a hill, in the last days of March, was a bleached-out, hippie Santa Claus! How could any of this be real?

"Um, um…," she stammered and put her hand to her forehead.

"You *did* come here looking for me, didn't you?" he asked, his ice-blue eyes peering over his glasses.

"No, I just…" Karina gestured lamely toward the bridge. She was so confused she could barely speak.

"Well, that's all right," said the man. "Please, come." He waved her forward. "I've got your paperwork right here. Just have a seat, and we'll get started."

"Paperwork?" Karina looked perplexed. She glanced back at the foot bridge and considered making a run for it. When she turned back to face him, the man was staring down at her. Karina took a tentative step forward, desperate to gauge this exceedingly odd man in this exceedingly odd place.

When she got within a few feet of him, she realized that what she'd taken for an altar was actually a massive block of ice chiseled with swirling shapes and patterns, which he was using as a desk. He motioned for her to take a seat in the simple wooden chair in front of it.

Karina edged toward the chair and sat down, deeply unsure of her presence here with this stranger. She put her hand hard to her cheek: Am I dreaming? Am I actually at home in bed? Is the alarm about to go off to wake me up for school? She paused for a moment in anticipation, but no alarm went off and she didn't wake up. Instead, she remained in this cave of ice waiting for this man to tell her what the hell was going on.

He returned to his place behind the desk.

"Now, let us begin at the beginning, shall we?" he said with a brusque, administrative smile. He picked up a fountain pen from the desktop. "Name?" he asked, his voice echoing against the cave walls. He held the pen ready to record her answer in a large leather-bound book.

"Um, Karina," she said, her brows knitted up in confusion. As he scribbled her name, she stared at the top of his hat and felt the absurdity of the situation wash over her. She grasped the arms of the chair and willed her mouth to form words. "Do you *live* here?" she asked. The man raised an eyebrow, then carefully set down the pen. He clasped his hands together on the desk.

"I am here, that is all I know. I have no recollection of how I got here or of my birth into this world." After a moment, he picked up the pen and resumed writing in the book. Karina sat in stunned silence. "But that is not unusual, is it?" he added, under his breath. Karina thought she saw the slightest hint of a smile on his lips. "Date of birth?" he asked, without looking up.

"Uh, August 22, 198…" The man stopped her with a slight wave of his hand.

"No, no, my dear. Do you *recall* the date of your birth? Do you remember it?" He gazed benignly at her as if this question weren't completely ridiculous.

"Uh, no," she answered. Her voice had the same edge it had whenever she was asked a stupid question.

"As I said—not at all unusual. And yet that is part of our problem, is it not? We are born and we forget, we live and we forget, and then we die and we forget." He leaned back in his chair and leveled his eyes at her.

"I… guess so," she said, beginning to suspect this cave-dweller wasn't entirely in his right mind. She studied him warily, scanning her memory for reports of crazy people on the loose. No, that wasn't it. This old guy might be weird, but he wasn't crazy. Well then, she demanded of herself, who was he and why was he here? What did he eat? Had he ever been outside this bizarre cave?

"And then we start over," he said. There was that strange little smile again.

"Huh?" said Karina, trying not to sound too ignorant, though she had clearly lost the thread of what he was saying.

She was, of course, a very intelligent girl, had the test scores to prove it. She understood most things, was capable of all manner of abstract thought, and had spent her fair share of time pondering the deeper mysteries of life. But this man was not making a bit of sense. She stared impatiently at him as he turned to a pocket at the back of the book and pulled out a sheet of paper. He briefly consulted it and again peered over his glasses at her.

"Ah, you are the beautiful—but damaged—Scarina, yes?" he asked. She'd hardly had a chance to wince at this name before she was overcome by astonishment that he should know it.

"How…?" She glanced around uncomfortably and continued, "…do you know that?"

"When the student is ready, the teacher appears," he said. She felt the heat rise in her cheeks. Did he think this was some kind of freaking joke? Who the hell did he think he was calling her that? Were The Bitches behind this whole thing?

She was opening her mouth to demand an explanation, when he slammed the book shut, the sound reverberating off the cave walls. He took off his glasses and turned his intense gaze upon her. He seemed to see right through her—though not in a threatening or accusing sort of way. On the contrary, as Karina sat across the desk from him, she felt acknowledged, appreciated, understood. As much as she wanted to curse this man and leave, there was something about him that compelled her to stay.

She was just beginning to feel uncomfortable with the silence, when he stood up and reached his hand across the desk.

"How do you do, Karina?" A smile suddenly burst forth from his cheeks. "I am Algernon." Despite his strange appearance—and the creepy fact that he knew too much about her—Karina decided to give him the benefit of the doubt.

Chapter 6

The icy walls of the cave gave the air a strange hollow feeling. Karina sat there staring at the man's hand and imagined she could hear the seconds ticking by. Though still somewhat naive about the world, she had learned that, sometimes, when in the presence of a stranger, her stomach would begin to feel sickly, as if a dark cloud had formed there. There had been occasions when she'd ignored this feeling, but usually she allowed it to lead her away from a person or situation. The handful of times she'd refused its warning, she'd ended up regretting it. Through trial and error, she'd come to trust her stomach's warning. Looking at this man now, she noticed a distinct lack of this feeling and just knew he was not a threat. She stood and placed her hand in his.

"Well done!" he said, shaking it with childlike enthusiasm. He stepped out from behind the desk, a smile crinkling the corners of his eyes. She blinked, puzzled by his congratulations. "The first step is learning to listen to yourself," he said, holding up a knobby finger. "Lovely, lovely!" he said. He stood there grinning for a moment, then nodded. "There's something I'd like to show you, if you are amenable."

"Um, okay," she said.

"If you would kindly step over here." He motioned for her to follow him around the desk.

With a gentle touch of her arm, he guided her to the soaring floor-to-ceiling window along the back wall of the cave. The brilliant stained-glass patterns on its surface were stunning. As he positioned her in front of it, she was startled to see the patterns begin to ripple and dissolve. After a moment, what had been opaque and glowing became reflective, and Karina found herself standing in front of a mirror—not exactly her favorite place to be.

"Do you see?" asked the man taking up a position next to her. She glanced at him impatiently.

"I see myself, if that's what you mean," Karina answered. She grimaced uncomfortably at her reflection and instinctively reached up to pull her bangs down over her forehead. She started to wonder if she'd been wrong to like him. Why was he so damn happy, anyway? Was he some kind of idiot? She concluded that his friendliness must mean that he hadn't yet noticed her scar.

"Look closely," he said. Sighing, she returned her

gaze to the mirror, clearly unimpressed by what she saw. There, as always, were the same old cheeks, the same old nose, mouth, and eyes. It was the same old face that always met her in the mirror.

She shifted on her feet and opened her mouth to ask him what she was supposed to be gaining from this exercise, when something in the mirror caught her eye. Behind her, a blurry mass grew up and began to move. She whipped around to see what it was, but there was nothing there. When she turned back toward the mirror, though, she saw it again.

Her first thought was that it must be her shadow, but it had color and was altogether the wrong shape. For a moment, she stood there waiting for it stop moving. When she cocked her head to one side to try to get a better view, it suddenly came into focus, and what she saw sucked the air right out of her lungs. Reflected in this fantastical window-mirror was a long line of people stretching out behind her.

Directly behind her was a prim woman with dark hair and pointy glasses, who looked as if she might be a school teacher or librarian. She was wearing a plaid skirt and a white blouse buttoned to the neck. Behind her was a tall, thin man with a mustache. He was dressed in a baggy brown suit and fedora and holding himself up with a silver-handled cane. Next was a man wearing a military uniform who looked as if he could be from World War I. Though he was farther back than the first two, Karina could plainly see the haunted look on his face. Behind him, a portly woman with a big nose and a sour expression was wearing a nun's habit. The motley assortment of people continued on into the distance.

Completely stumped as to what it could mean, Karina stared at this bizarre conga line behind her. She looked at Algernon in the mirror, hoping he might provide an explanation. Instead, he just smiled. There didn't appear to be anyone standing behind him. When she turned back to her own reflection, she noticed that the movement of her head rippled down the line of people, as if they were puppets and she held the strings. She raised an arm and let out a strained chuckle as, one by one, they raised theirs.

She looked more closely at the person directly behind her, the librarian, and studied her shy, gentle face. She peered into the woman's eyes and felt a sudden shock of recognition. Karina was sure she'd never seen this woman before, but when she looked into her face, she saw her own eyes gazing back at her.

Slowly it began to dawn on her that this woman was some alternate version of herself. It was a strange, uncomfortable feeling. She was Karina and yet not Karina

—but of her identity there could be no doubt. The same thing happened when she looked at the next person and the next. Each one gazed back at her with her own eyes.

"Who are they?" asked Karina, though she felt she already knew the answer.

"Do you recognize any of them?"

"They kind of look like… me," she said.

"That's right!" he said. He turned to pat her on the shoulder. "Excellent." Karina stepped back from the mirror, her mind flashing with strange thoughts and images. "Now, I do believe you must be going my dear. It's quite late, you know," he said, gesturing toward the tunnel. They began to make their way along the stream. Karina wanted to ask him so many questions but didn't want to be rude or overstay her welcome.

"Tell me, Karina, what do you see in *my* eyes?" he asked, stopping near the water's edge. He leaned forward and opened his eyes wide so she could get a good look. Although she was more or less convinced by now that this man was neither crazy nor dangerous, she was nevertheless uncomfortable being so close to him. Still, she consented to peer into his eyes and decided that they were honest and perceived much.

"You seem friendly? I mean, I can tell you're a nice person."

"Outstanding! The eyes are the windows to the soul, as they say. And you know that if I meant you any harm, you would see it in my eyes. You would get a feeling right here," he said, touching his stomach, "warning you not to trust me."

"Yeah," she said slowly. How did he know about the cloud in her tummy?

"Karina," he said, placing a hand on her shoulder, "I can tell you're going to be an excellent pupil. There are many things you must learn about the world in order to be happy in it. It can be a very challenging place—one of the most challenging, in fact." She frowned, not sure what he meant by this, but before she could say anything, he continued. "It's true that you are sometimes unhappy?"

Karina felt suddenly defensive, as if she'd been accused of a crime. No, she wasn't unhappy, not in the usual sense of the word. She knew what it was to be unhappy; her cousin, Lily, had struggled with depression for years. It had gotten so bad that her parents had taken her to a facility. When she'd gotten out two months later, the doctors had given her a bunch of pills to stop her from crying all day. No, Karina wasn't depressed. This man was just wrong.

"I wouldn't say that," she said, her chin in the air.

"Then you are happy," he asked, glancing away.

Karina paused to consider the question.

"Well, sometimes, yeah. When something good happens, I'm happy."

"And the rest of the time?"

"I'm just… nothing, I guess. Somewhere between happy and sad. Just kind of there." She looked dismayed by the words coming out of her own mouth.

"Exactly! That is the human condition, you see." His smile seemed at odds with the look in his eye. "To find ourselves here on this Earth, with no recollection of our origins; to experience passing joy, passing pain; to wonder about our purpose; to mourn the past and worry about the future; to be often uneasy; to be at the mercy of events we cannot control; to long for love; to feel as if there is always something missing—though we know not what. To feel frustrated that we cannot get what we want, and when we do get it, to find that it does not fulfill us."

Karina nodded, more to herself than to him. As she stared at the ground digesting his words, she heard the sound of singing coming from a hole in the frozen stream.

> *"How many lives have I lived in this hole,*
> *Swimming and kicking my feet?*
> *No one can know the depths of his soul,*
> *'Til his watery journey's complete."*

She approached the hole and saw a huge, rainbow-colored fish. Sparks emanated from its swishing tail as it swam, and its undulating body made it seem to vanish and reappear. Its strange, otherworldly beauty and flashing tail were mesmerizing. When the fish made a turn, Karina thought she could see the entire cave reflected in each tiny, prismatic scale.

"Oh, there's a fish," she said.

As if on cue, the fish leaped out of the water and landed squarely in Karina's arms. Startled, she fumbled with it, almost getting it under control only to repeatedly lose her grip. She gave Algernon a pleading look, but he just smiled and looked unsurprised.

When she finally got ahold of the fish, it settled down and began to gasp, its mouth and gills opening and closing spasmodically. It turned its head to examine her with one giant, bulging fish eye. Karina was stunned to see that its face was closer to a man's than a fish's. Her eyes settled on the creature's large, puckered lips, and she found it impossible to look away. Only when they began to form words was she delivered from her trance.

"Hello, love!" said the fish in a posh British accent. Karina stifled a laugh. "I'm glad you're here. Do you know why?"

"No. Is it because you feel like you're going crazy

in here, too?" she asked.

"Oh, you're not crazy, lass. Although, to see into the nature of things can certainly make one feel as if one is going mad." He attempted to wriggle free from her grasp, then continued. "But that is not what I meant. Do you know why you are here?"

"Um, no." Karina felt a little absurd talking to a fish. She gestured toward the foot bridge. "I just found this weird door in the hillside, and I…"

"No, Karina! Do you know why you are here in this world? Do you know why you wear this body, why you were born?" Again nonsensical questions were being put to her. She searched herself for an answer but felt as if she were being asked to solve an unsolvable riddle.

Riveted by his bizarre fish-man lips, Karina replayed in her mind the events leading up to her discovery of the cave. She'd been walking with Henry before she found the door—of that much she was sure. Had she fallen somewhere along the trail and hit her head? Was she presently lying on the ground having a seizure? Had she breathed in more of the neighbor's pot smoke than she realized? Try as she might, she couldn't convince herself that she wasn't experiencing some sort of monumental hallucination.

When the fish again wriggled in her arms, Karina

came back to herself and glanced at Algernon for a clue as to how to respond, only to see that he, too, was waiting for an answer.

"No. I don't." She sounded annoyed. "I don't remember how I got here or how I was born. I don't remember most of what happened to me as a baby. It's kind of like I've always been here. In fact, I can't remember *not* being here."

"Then you must re*mem*ber!" said the fish.

"How am I supposed to do that?" she asked, exasperated.

"By becoming acquainted with yourself," said the fish calmly. "By finding out what you have hidden from yourself. You must find out who you truly are." The absurdity of this imperative made her fidget. She knew who she was. She was Karina, damn it!

The fish wriggled valiantly, forcing her to reassert her mastery over him. He stared at her with one wild eye, then settled down again.

"To be, or not to be—that is the question. But perhaps the question ought to be: To be and to be and to be," said the fish. He began humming to himself, and his eyes spun in their sockets. Karina felt a wave of irritation crest inside her.

"Do you know who *you* are?" she demanded.

"But, of course! I have cleansed myself, and now I am whole," answered the fish, waving a melodramatic fin in the air. The fish's answer conjured up the memory of a camping trip she'd taken with her family to Emerald Lake. An image ran through her mind of her father crouched by the water's edge gutting a trout, chopping off its head and tail, and rinsing it in the clear lake water.

"Are you a man or a fish?" she asked. The fish's lips formed a deep, enigmatic smile.

"I am awake!" he said, finally wriggling free of her grasp and leaping back into the hole. Chuckling, Karina shook her head and dried her hands on her shirt. When she looked back at the hole, she saw the fish floating on its side.

"Oh my God. Is he…?" asked Karina, fearing she'd kept him out of the water too long.

"Oh, don't worry. He does that all the time," said Algernon, with a dismissive wave of his hand. The fish let out a maniacal giggle and disappeared beneath the surface. Karina sighed.

"I really…"

"…should be going," he said. She stepped onto the foot bridge and turned to face him. "Whenever you need us, we'll be here." She heard a splash and glanced down at the hole, where the fish was swimming and singing.

"The excellent maiden Karina,
Found a door with a handle of brass.
And saw all of those who had been her
Reflected in the looking glass."

Chapter 7

Karina emerged from the tunnel, stomping her feet to free the ice from her shoes. She glanced up and down the creek bed but could see no one in the light of the hazy moon. The rocks, slippery with dew, forced her to take care with each step as she headed back toward the trail. She felt drained and fuzzy, as if waking from a dream, and knew that what she had just experienced stood well outside the ordinary realm. An old man in a frozen cave? A talking fish? No, she reasoned with herself, it must have been something other than what it seemed. She must have fallen asleep. That was the most logical explanation.

And yet, somehow, the cave and its inhabitants felt *more* real than her everyday reality—extra-real, hyper-real. In there, everything seemed to have an added layer of meaning and significance. It was as if she'd been able to step outside her reality and look back on it, take in its greater breadth and outline. She knew in her heart that she'd been given a rare opportunity to go beyond her usual vantage point and see her life in a way that was impossible while trapped within it. She felt special, blessed—as if she'd stumbled upon a truly transcendent experience. It was either that, she thought, or she was slobberingly mad and would presently be hauled off to a psych ward.

When she reached the backyard, Karina noticed that the neighbor boy hadn't moved from his spot. How long have I been gone? she wondered. It certainly *felt* like a long time—hours maybe.

As she stood there watching this boy sitting in the dim circle of light from his back patio, she was struck by the strange realization that she knew things about him. Suddenly, inexplicably, she was able to perceive all kinds of things about him. Even from a distance, his aching loneliness was obvious. And though she'd never given him much thought, as she stood there looking at him now, she felt things about him she had no real way of knowing.

She saw that he was alone most of the time and that when his mother was there, she was a sickly, drugged-out mess. Calling to mind the only time she'd ever seen his mother, Karina realized that the way she'd looked then fit with this new understanding. She was also able to pick up that his father had been abusive and that was why his mother had kicked him out. She saw how he struggled in school and how the shame he felt about his home life caused him to shy away from people. And somehow—though she didn't know how—she was able to gather all this from a single, brief glance in the darkness.

Karina had always wondered what made this boy so awkward and, to quote The Bitches, "vomit-worthy." But now she felt she knew exactly why he was the way he was. She couldn't remember how long they'd been neighbors, but until this moment, she'd never understood—or even tried to understand—what was wrong with him. Now that she could see what he was facing, though, her long-standing revulsion toward him began to shift and dissolve. In its place, something new rushed in. It was compassion.

Just as she was turning to go inside, the boy lifted his head, as if suddenly aware someone had been watching him. He turned to look at her, and when their eyes met, she blushed, embarrassed to have been caught staring at him. She gave him an awkward smile. He looked startled, shot her a quick frown, and got up to go inside. Though it was not the response she'd been expecting, she shrugged and headed inside.

Exhausted, Karina lurched toward the lights of the house as if toward a beacon. She opened the sliding glass door and had the feeling of returning after traveling a great distance. Wherever she had been—real or imagined—

she'd somehow made it back. She told herself that *this* was real—the light, the house, the patio beneath her feet. Or at least it was what passed for reality in her ordinary, daily-grind world—so she'd might as well get used to it. She stepped inside and felt the warmth of the house wrap around her.

Henry ran up to greet her, his tail wagging.

"There you are!" Karina picked him up and stroked his back. She heard her brothers arguing upstairs and resolved to keep the cave a secret for the time being.

"Mom!" screamed Jonah, his words distorted by anger. "Max is flicking boogers at me again!"As she climbed the stairs toward the sound of splashing, she felt a curious combination of comfort and dread. At least this was familiar.

As she passed the open bathroom door, she caught sight of Jonah, who was standing in a cloud of steam next to the bath.

"Get out, you F-ing pus hole! I need to take a shower!" Jonah yelled at Max.

Before Karina could cross the doorway, though, she froze. Slowly, she turned to look at Jonah—the brother she'd known most of her life, who'd grown up alongside her, who'd occupied the same womb as her, and who'd always possessed a 100% normal anatomy—to see that he now had two heads. Or, more precisely, two faces.

For a moment, she stood in the hallway, waiting for her mind to sort out the grotesque mirage she saw before her. She attempted to focus her eyes, blinking and squinting in the hope that what she was seeing would resolve into something sensible. But this was not some trick of water and light, nor of fatigue. For reasons that were well beyond her comprehension, Jonah's face now had two distinct dimensions.

There was the usual face Jonah wore while arguing with Max—a hateful, pitiless grimace. This was his "real" face—the visible one, the one she was used to seeing. But now, superimposed upon this face—or underneath it, she couldn't tell which—was another face, this one filmy and transparent. On this strange "other" face, Jonah wore a different set of emotions—sadness, jealousy, pain. There, Karina could plainly see Jonah's deeper feelings toward Max, the ones no one else knew about—possibly not even him. Despite torturing Max on a nearly constant basis, Karina realized, Jonah didn't really hate him. This ghostly other face told her that, deep down, Jonah felt rejected by Max and longed for his approval.

In a flash of insight into her brothers' never-ending struggle, Karina saw another, older layer to their relationship. At an earlier time, which she could only conclude was a previous life, Jonah had been Max's son. In that life, Max had been the aggressor and had inflicted a wound so deep that it had survived even death. Though Max had worked tirelessly to put food on the table, like many men of an earlier generation, he'd been emotionally absent. The burden of earning a living had hardened him and made him ambivalent toward his family. And although all his children had been wounded by his neglect, Jonah, the youngest, had been hurt the most by it and had never forgiven him.

Reeling from this bizarre vision, Karina continued down the hall to her room and shut the door behind her. She stood in front of her desk and stared at the wall for a while, trying to process what she'd just seen. Clearly something way out of the ordinary was happening to her.

She sat down slowly and put her head in her hands. Was she crazy? Sick? It didn't feel like it. What it did feel like, though, was that she'd seen Jonah more clearly, more deeply, than she'd ever been able to before. Finally, she felt as if she had some insight into her brothers' bitter rivalry. This was an old pain, an old hurt— she was sure of it. And as she sat there turning it over in her mind, she couldn't help but wonder if their struggle might never end.

Chapter 8

"TGIFF. Am I right, people?" said Mr. Stratton, as the students opened their notebooks. "The extra 'F' standing, of course, for 'fantabulous,'" he added dryly. A pudgy girl with glasses in the front row burst out laughing.

As Mr. Stratton delved into the history of psychoanalysis, Karina sat there wondering what to make of the previous night's experience. Her first impulse upon waking had been to run down to the creek to confirm that the door, the cave, Algernon, and the fish were, in fact, real. She'd even set her alarm clock 15 minutes early, hoping to sneak out before anyone else got up, but had hit the snooze button and lost her chance.

"...led to his discovery of the unconscious," Mr. Stratton was saying. "Because of this paradigm-shifting discovery, Freud changed the way the modern era—the period beginning with his own Victorian age—thought about the mind."

Mr. Stratton was young for a teacher, tall and

muscular with golden brown hair that grew past his ears. His intense blue eyes had just enough gleam in them to make him seem slightly dangerous. He was what The Bs called "sexy." On the blackboard he'd scrawled the words "id," "ego," and "superego."

"Then there was Freud's successor, Carl Jung. Freud, who had been trained as a medical doctor, viewed the unconscious from a scientific perspective, while his pupil, Jung, immersed himself in Eastern philosophy and approached the mind from a more… spiritual point of view. Where Freud was cerebral, Jung was visceral," he said, pointing to his abs. The pudgy girl swooned.

"But despite their differences," said Mr. Stratton, "there was one thing they shared—and this is the important part, Cunningham—," he said, cocking an eyebrow at a skateboarder dozing off in the back, "…a belief in the unconscious." He wrote down the word and underlined it twice.

"Both men were convinced that everything that ever happened to a person—every thought, every deed, from the moment of birth to the moment of death—was recorded in the subconscious. And they endeavored to prove their theory by placing their patients into a hypnotic —Jung would have said 'meditative'—state and encouraging them to recall the repressed memories they believed were the cause of disease."

"Do you recall your birth?" Karina heard Algernon's voice in her head. Perhaps the question wasn't so ridiculous after all. Was it really possible to remember that far back, to the dawning of consciousness, the very first breath? If she could put herself into the proper state of mind and allow her mind to relax, Karina wondered, might she actually be able to remember the first moments of life? There was only one way to find out.

Positioned as she was behind a large volleyball player, Karina closed her eyes, hoping Mr. Stratton wouldn't notice if, just for a minute, she performed a little experiment. After the prodding she'd received in the cave, Karina was anxious to put the theory to the test and see if she could remember something—anything. She slid down in her chair, focused on the sound of her breathing, and emptied her mind. Mr. Stratton's voice began to fade into the background. She relaxed and let darkness envelop her.

And then… nothing.

She waited and waited and before long became frustrated and impatient. She clenched her fists, trying to force her memory to return. When that didn't work, she called up one of her favorite childhood memories: the day her family had brought Henry home from the shelter. Though she'd been very young at the time, she'd never forgotten the way he'd licked her face in the backseat on the way home. She thought if she could use that moment as a point of reference, she might be able to reach back and retrieve something earlier. Her attempts to peer into that void, however, into the dawning days of her life, failed.

She thought about the portrait hanging in the hallway outside her bedroom. It was a photo of her in a frilly, lilac-colored dress taken a few months before her fall. Though she passed it several times a day, it recorded a moment in time she just couldn't remember.

After a few more minutes of trying, Karina was starting to think it was impossible to retrieve a memory from that far back. She was just about to give up, when the darkness behind her eyelids suddenly lifted, and the image of a white room filled her mind. She had only a vague sense that it was white, though, because the harsh light was stabbing into her eyes, making it impossible to see.

Behind this cold, oppressive light, Karina could hear strange clanging noises while the air pricked at her skin. She thought she heard voices, but the words were unintelligible, as if spoken underwater. A dreadful combination of fear, confusion, and exhaustion gripped her, and though she was struck by the urge to cry, she could barely manage a gasp.

As she struggled to make sense of where she was,

a figure bent over her, partially blocking the light from above. Though Karina couldn't make out the person's features, she had the sense that it was a woman.

The next thing she knew, she felt a rush of movement and a strong sense of vertigo as the frigid air swished around her. She instinctively reached out to steady herself, but her arms flailed uselessly. After a few seconds, the room stopped spinning, and she was laid down on something cold and hard, after which a gooey, burning substance was smeared into her eyes. She struggled to breathe and to see and felt as if she were being tortured.

Terror overwhelmed her, and she finally let out a desperate cry. After a few long moments, during which she was tossed around and had no idea what was being done to her, she was deposited onto a soft, moist bed. She felt instantly soothed and sensed the warmth and safety of this place. The spinning room slowed to a stop, and she heard a tender voice in her ear.

The voice seemed like something out of a dream, as if it were reaching her from a long distance, though she was not sure whether that distance was one of time or of space. It seemed as if it had been approaching her for a long time, slowly increasing in volume until it had finally arrived. Everything about it was familiar, and she strained to listen. For a moment, she tried to focus her eyes on her surroundings but gave up and collapsed back onto this bed, where everything—the smell, the sound, the dewy warmth —was comforting.

"Hello, Karina," whispered the voice. "Happy Birthday." It was her mother; she'd remembered!

Riiiiiiiing! Karina was suddenly back in the classroom, her mother's voice echoing in her ears as the classroom erupted in movement.

"Neuroses next week, people!" Mr. Stratton was shouting over the commotion of backpacks being zipped up and chairs being slid across the floor. Karina slowly pulled herself up and began gathering her things. She glanced around at Mr. Stratton and the other students, but no one seemed to have any idea about the incredible thing that had just happened to her.

In a daze, she picked up her backpack and drifted toward the door. She stepped into the hallway and smack into the path of The Bs. As they strode toward her on their sharp, spiky heels, Karina started to panic. She surveyed possible avenues of escape but quickly concluded that there were none. Realizing she was trapped, she dropped her head and made an effort to shrink into the wall behind her. A second later, they were upon her. With no teachers or any sign of Mary Blair, there would be no defense against their onslaught. There was nothing left to do but brace for impact. She held her breath and cowered against the wall.

A moment later, she opened her eyes and saw something that completely blew her mind. After months and months of brutal, degrading torment, Karina had come to accept that bullying was just part of her life. But today The Bs did something she couldn't have anticipated if she'd suffered through a thousand Bitchy attacks: They ignored her.

When they were at their closest point, Emma turned to glance briefly in Karina's direction but never even broke stride. It was as if she'd been rendered momentarily invisible. She was still standing there, her mouth hanging open, when The Bs rounded the corner, never once looking back.

"Oh my God," she said under her breath. A second unbelievable thing had just happened in the space of ten minutes. For reasons she couldn't begin to fathom, something had just occurred that she'd never dreamed possible: The Bitches had left her alone. After checking her arms and legs to confirm she was indeed visible, a slow, furtive smile crept onto her face. Had she just crossed into some alternate universe, one in which she was allowed to exist without a daily helping of torture? The day had just shot to the top of her list of Best Days Ever.

Stifling a celebratory yelp, Karina made her way through the crush of students to her locker at the end of the hall. There, Principal Sadler, a middle-aged woman whose love of discipline was constantly under attack by the students of Vista Verde, was giving someone the business. When she got closer, she realized it was Mary Blair.

In a business suit cut for a considerably thinner woman, Principal Sadler had Mary Blair pinned against the wall. The principal's clenched fists were jammed into her hips, and her swollen, red face was spitting words. Mary Blair, in a cringing pose similar to the one in which Karina herself had just been, was flinching, grimacing, and trying not to meet her gaze.

"…late to class again! This is your last warning, do you understand?" shouted Principal Sadler, waving her fat little finger in the air.

"That's not true. I was there. She just didn't see me," Mary Blair pleaded. The principal snorted, then leaned in to sniff her. Her flared nostrils underscored her already-uncanny resemblance to a bulldog. She recoiled with a scowl.

"Have you been smoking?" she demanded.

"No, I swear," Mary Blair protested emphatically to the floor.

Karina finished at her locker, quietly closed the door, and inched toward them. Spying Karina out of the corner of her eye, Mary Blair gave her a barely perceptible wave. When she was a few feet away, Karina dropped to her knee, pretending to tie her shoe as a cover for her eavesdropping.

When she glanced up at Principal Sadler, she was so startled by what she saw, she let out an audible grunt and almost toppled backward. Now it was the principal who had grown another face! Karina blinked a few times, but when she looked again, Principal Sadler's "other" face was even more apparent.

For all the spite she was unloading onto Mary Blair, Principal Sadler's other face was even angrier. The main difference seemed to be that where her physical face was critical of everyone around her, her other face was critical—unmercifully, unrelentingly critical—of herself.

On this other face, Karina saw the self-hatred born of a lifetime of fractured career plans, failed romances, and forgotten hopes. The course her life had taken had left her seething with the disgust and resentment she took out on those around her. The mental anguish she put herself through on a daily basis was so fiendishly cruel, Karina couldn't help but feel sorry for her. Looking at her now, she understood why most of the students—and some of the staff—hated her so much. Life had left her utterly heartbroken.

"…you got that?" Principal Sadler was saying.

"Yeah." Mary Blair nodded, desperate to put an end to the spit shower she was receiving.

"Good," said the two-headed principal, yanking her jacket sleeves down over her wrists and curling her lip in one last disapproving snarl. She whipped around, glared at Karina, and thundered off down the hall. Karina stared until she was out of sight.

"Dude," said Mary Blair, rolling her eyes. "I got detention *again*!" Karina grabbed her backpack and got to her feet.

"That blows," she said, as they started down the hallway. "What happened?"

"Mrs. Wronkowitz totally lied and said I was late to class. Hate that bitch!" she said. Though nothing in her words or expression revealed it, Karina just knew her friend had, in fact, been late.

"Were you?" she asked.

"Hell-a-men-*no*!"

Karina had always trusted Mary Blair and never dreamed that her best friend would lie to her. But faced with the near-certainty that she was lying, Karina couldn't help but wonder what else she might've lied about.

Her friend lying to her so easily, so casually, was like a knife to the ribs. And the fact that she would lie about something so dumb (Karina didn't care if she was late) added a layer of confusion to the hurt. She was starting to think her strange new powers might not be such a good thing after all.

Karina stopped in the middle of the hallway, unsure how to proceed in light of this BFF-code breach. She was opening her mouth to ask Mary Blair why she would lie, when it dawned on her that she might not even realize she was doing it.

When Mary Blair noticed that Karina had stopped, she turned to see what was holding her up and caught the hard look in her eye.

"What's the matter?" she asked. Karina stared blankly at her. "C'mon! I don't want to be late for art, too," she said, continuing down the hallway. The thought that Mary Blair half-believed what she was saying—that she was lying to herself as much as to Karina—made overlooking her fib a little easier. She decided to drop it and hurried to catch up.

The girls arrived at the door to the art room, and Karina waited for Mary Blair to speak, hoping that the next words out of her mouth would be true.

"I am so boned, dude. I have this giant art project

due Monday." Mary Blair threw back her head and groaned. "We're supposed to paint something that has 'meaning' to us, and I spent all week working on this one thing, but it turned out to be super-lame. I just can't…." She squinted, grasping at the air in front of her.

For Karina, this quintessentially Mary Blair gesture summed up her entire personality. As she watched her do it now, she was reminded of the very first time she'd seen it. Within five minutes of laying eyes on her, Karina had known they would be friends.

It had been a few days into the new school year. Karina had been spending the break between classes in the usual way: peering into her locker mirror and trying to pull her bangs down over her forehead. She'd arranged them as best as she could and was closing the door, when she heard Commander Bitch Avery's barbed-wire voice in her ear.

"You're wasting your time, Scarface." Karina had spun around to see Avery and The Bs fanned out in front of her, designer clothes dripping from their perfectly proportioned bodies. Striking ridiculous fashion-magazine poses, they'd taken turns looking her up and down. The disgust radiating off their pursed red lips had made Karina wish she could squeeze into her locker and shut the door. "It doesn't matter what you do, you're always going to be hideous. You should just give up," Avery had said loudly enough for everyone in the hallway to hear. Stifled laughter had rippled down the row of students standing by their lockers.

Karina had been on the verge of tears, when a distracted Mary Blair had come flailing around the corner, almost knocking Amanda off her high heels. When The Bs had seen her eccentric mismatched outfit and frizzy braided hair, they'd gasped melodramatically. Clutching at one another with their perfectly manicured nails, they'd clomped on their heels like frightened thoroughbreds.

"Oh my Gaaaawd!" Avery had said, glancing between Karina and this odd new person. "The ugly's catching! Scarina's contagious! Run, you guys! Run for your lives!" she'd shrieked in mock terror. The Bs had taken off down the hall, laughing obnoxiously all the way to the end.

Karina had blinked a few times at her soon-to-be best friend, not quite sure what to make of her. Underneath the relief that she'd shown up when she did was a slight twinge of fear. Karina had never seen anyone—especially not at Verde Vista—who looked anything like Mary Blair. She was different, unique, fascinating.

"I think it's cool," she'd said, opening her locker.

"Huh?" Karina had asked, discretely checking out her outfit.

"Your scar—it's kind of…," Mary Blair had said, performing her signature grasping-at-the-air move, "… hardcore. I mean, Harry Potter's got one, right?" she'd said, smiling. By the end of the week, they were spending every spare second together.

A gentle thwack on the arm brought Karina back to the present. Mary Blair was frowning at her.

"What're you doing this weekend?" Karina asked.

"Nothing."

"Can you sleep over tomorrow?"

"Sure."

"Good. There's something I want to show you." Karina flashed a quick grin, spun on her heels, and headed down the hallway.

"What?" called out Mary Blair. "What!?" Instead of answering, though, Karina turned to wave coquettishly over her shoulder, as Mary Blair scowled her way through the art room door.

Chapter 9

When Karina arrived home that afternoon, she was feeling pretty good. Excited about the sleepover, she hurried inside to clear it with her mom. She bounded into the kitchen to find her standing at the counter sifting through a pile of mail.

"Hi, honey," her mom said without looking up. Despite the fact that her mother looked the way she always did at the end of a work day—same slumped posture, same dark circles under her eyes—Karina knew immediately something was wrong.

"Hey," she said, dropping her backpack. "Is everything alright?"

"Yeah, of course. Why?"

"I dunno," said Karina, glancing at the envelope in her hand. "What's that?"

"Nothing," she said, tucking it into the pile. Karina was suddenly struck by the same feeling she'd had talking to Mary Blair earlier and just knew she'd been lied to—

this time by her own mother.

Karina wasn't stupid, of course. She knew people told lies. She'd read somewhere that most people lied several times a day and some several times an hour. She understood *intellectually* that people lied, but she couldn't help but be hurt when someone did it to her. It was a shock —like a sudden, unprovoked slap. And no matter how she tried to understand the reasons someone might lie, it always felt like a vote of no confidence—a declaration that she wasn't cool enough or trustworthy enough or grown up enough to be granted the truth.

Nevertheless, Karina had to admit that she herself sometimes lied. There were times when there seemed no way around it, like when her father asked her if he looked fat. She knew he didn't really want to hear the truth. At times like that, it was just easier to lie than to tell him he looked six month's pregnant. And she was pretty sure it was easier for her father that way, too. To Karina's mind, this kind of lie wasn't really *bad*. It was a lie of love—if there could be such a thing.

This new talent for being able to tell when people were lying, to observe the thoughts occurring inside their heads and plainly see how those thoughts contradicted their words, left Karina wondering how to react. It put her in an awkward position, because the person doing the lying—in this case her mother—assumed that she was believed. Was she supposed to call people out on it? Or just let them believe their lies had gone undetected? She consoled herself with the thought that it was better to know when someone was lying than to not know. But she felt uncomfortable being in possession of such information. What if she didn't *want* to know?

She stood there looking at her mother, the last person she'd suspect of intentionally deceiving her, pretending that the letter she'd just received wasn't bad news. No sooner had she begun to wonder what it was about, than the answer began to filter into her mind. Though it was warm and stuff in the kitchen, Karina felt suddenly cold and withered inside, and a darkness took hold of her chest. Somehow, she was certain it had something to do with Gram.

Despite the age difference between them, Karina and her grandmother had always shared a remarkably deep bond. Everyone in the family knew how much they meant to each other. They had a lot in common: a love of great stories, an attraction to offbeat subjects, a curiosity about what made people tick. They were what Gram called "simpatico." As she stood there in the kitchen, Karina knew that the ache in her chest meant that whatever was in that envelope was going to make her very, very sad. She decided to leave well enough alone and allow her mother's lie to stand.

She turned toward the patio door but then remembered the sleepover. "Hey, Mom. Can Mary Blair spend the night tomorrow? Please?"

"Uh, sure."

"Thanks," said Karina, sliding open the door. She shook off her concern for Gram and stepped out into the late afternoon sun. She was excited to return to the cave and wanted to do some fact-checking before Mary Blair came over. She didn't want to look like an idiot in front of her friend.

She made her way down the trail and quickly found the spot where the door had been. She was surprised to see that the branches had regrown overnight and began tugging at them, peering beneath the leaves until—yes, there it was! It hadn't been a dream. There really was a door there.

After a few moments of struggling with the branches, Karina uncovered the door and was almost as startled by it as she had been the first time. Everything about this door was different. It looked brand new, as if it had just been installed, and the wood gleamed with a fresh coat of varnish. Even in the shade of the embankment, the fine brass handle shone like gold. She ran her hand along the smooth wood. Could there be a second entrance to the cave? Or perhaps a second cave? Surely that was not possible. But then, everything about this cave was impossible, so why not two impossible caves?

Karina stepped back to examine the embankment and confirm that this was indeed the place she'd entered before. She approached the door again and grabbed the handle. The latch clicked easily this time, as if it had been recently oiled.

She opened the door and peered inside to find that the tunnel, too, was changed. Although it was dark, Karina could clearly see that the floor was now covered in smooth stepping stones with grass sprouting up between them. The mossy, earthen walls were being held back by the roots of trees, some of which had leaves sprouting from them. Karina paused for a moment and imagined she could feel the roots' heartbeat. This tunnel is alive! she thought.

As she began to make her way down, the smell of vegetation swirled around her. When she was almost to the end, she bent down to remove a pebble that had become lodged in the tread of her sneaker. When she stood up, Algernon was standing on the bridge in front of her.

"Well, hello, Karina. Glad you could make it," he said as he stepped aside to reveal the radically transformed cave. She joined him on the bridge, her mouth hanging open. What had been cold and dead was now warm and pulsatingly alive.

The walls of the cave were covered in vines and branches, and the formerly frozen stream burbled merrily. Everywhere she looked, springtime flowers burst from their beds. There were small buds, large blooms, exotic bouquets—thousands of flowers of every imaginable color and shade.

The air was thick with perfume and the buzzing of bees, while birds flitted from tree to tree, warbling their peaceful contentment. Some perched in the trees, flashing their brilliant wings, while others swooped down to land on the lush grass before her. She gazed over the bridge at the rocks in the stream and noticed that they were polished to gemstone perfection.

When she finally turned her attention to Algernon, Karina saw that he, too, had been transformed. Although clearly the same person, he appeared decades younger, his white coat replaced by brocade vestments embroidered in green and gold. Gone was his straggly white beard, in its place a neatly cropped brown one. His eyes brimmed with vitality, and the wrinkles that had made him appear so wise before were barely perceptible. Somehow, it seemed, he had aged backward.

Karina fought her way through awestruck amazement to find her voice.

"You look different," she said.

"Do I?" He glanced down at himself. "Yes, I suppose I do." Though his appearance had completely changed, his voice was the same. He clasped his hands behind his back and waited for her to speak.

"So, this is real, right?" she asked, as they stepped off the bridge together. "I didn't make this place up?"

"Oh, no. You didn't make it up—not in the usual sense of the word. It's very real indeed." He glanced around admiringly and breathed in the sweet-smelling air.

"Okay, then," she said, facing him. "I need to ask you a few questions."

"Fire away."

"Okay." She cleared her throat. "Ever since last night, some really weird stuff has been happening. That... that was you, right?" she asked, her tone vaguely accusing. "Or this place?"

"Oh, no," he said. "That was all you."

"But it happened *because* of you and this place, right?" Karina was determined to find out why she could suddenly see two faces on people who had formerly had only one. And then there was the matter of her newly installed lie detector. She knew these things had to be related to her discovery of the cave and felt he owed her some kind of explanation.

"Yes. You have begun to perceive things that were hidden from you. This," he said, gesturing toward the cave, "is one of those things." She looked confused.

"So, are you *God* or something?" She shifted nervously on her feet. "Because I didn't use to, y'know, *believe* in God, but if you say you're God, then I totally believe you… I mean, *in* you… whatever."

"Oh, no." He shook his head. "No. I am Algernon." He laid a hand on his chest and bowed as if to introduce himself. "God is that which surpasses understanding. I am merely me. But thank you for the compliment," he said with a chuckle. Karina decided to drop the question of Algernon's identity and move on.

"What happened to the cave? Where's all the snow?"

"Have you not found yourself becoming more aware of certain things, things other people miss?" he asked, ambling toward the stream.

"Yeah," answered Karina, following him.

"Well, the cave reflects that change," he said. "You are evolving and so is the cave." He stopped and glanced down at the stream. Karina followed his gaze and watched as the water began to form an eddy. A moment later, a flower grew up out of it and blossomed into the air, the water beading off its graceful white petals. Though her knowledge of horticulture was limited, the thought entered Karina's mind that this was a lotus flower. He bent down to pluck it, then stood and handed it to her. "You see, this is *your* cave, my dear."

She smiled and took the flower, then held it up to her nose to drink in the intoxicating scent. She was about to thank him, when something in the center of the flower caught her eye. In the place where the stamen ought to have been was a sight that stole her breath away—an entire miniature universe!

At the center of this otherwise ordinary flower was a void as black as deepest space. There, Karina watched as planets drew perfect circles around their stars, bright-white galaxies churned endlessly, and massive, multicolored gas clouds formed brilliant, billowing shapes.

Karina stared at the infinity contained within this single bloom until her head began to hurt. When she felt herself being sucked into the void, she reeled backward and dropped the flower onto the grass. She covered her eyes, which burned from the light of all those stars.

Seemingly unaware of the careless way she'd discarded his gift, Algernon lifted Karina's chin and peered into her eyes the way a doctor might.

"Have you been remembering?" he asked.

"Yes, I… I remembered things and saw things… things that weren't there." She sounded embarrassed.

"You were seeing the essence of things. And of people." He let go of her chin. "This is a great gift."

"Something tells me it's going to get a lot worse before it gets better," she said, blinking.

"Only if you want it to," he replied, regarding her kindly. "And what about that?" he asked, pointing toward her forehead. "Have you remembered that?"

"What? My scar? No." she said, turning away from him. "And I'm not sure I want to. My mom said it was really bad."

"I understand. Sometimes the mind does not wish to remember things. But the body never forgets."

"Wouldn't it be better *not* to remember something like this?" she asked.

"It may be easier for the mind in the short term. But until the body recalls the pain caused by a wound, it cannot heal."

"But I *can't* remember! I'm telling you, I can't. Believe me, I've tried. How am I supposed to feel something if I can't…?"

Before she could finish speaking, a drop of blood trickled down her face. With trembling fingers, she reached up to touch her forehead. Her wound, which had long ago knitted up and been covered over by the scar that was the source of so much shame, was suddenly jagged and wet. The sting of her fingers on the open gash made her wince. Karina pulled back her hand and stared in disbelief at the blood on her fingertips.

When she turned to Algernon and saw the concerned look on his face, she began to panic. Her head started to pound, and the ground began to fluctuate beneath her feet. Before she could open her mouth to ask him what was happening, a spark surged from the tips of her bloody fingers to the deepest recesses of her brain, causing pain so acute her eyeballs rattled in their sockets.

She staggered under the weight of the feelings and images that came crashing down on her, and just like that, the entirety of her fall came back to her, every detail as clear as if it had occurred a moment earlier.

Under the warm afternoon sun, Karina finds herself in the backyard of her childhood home playing with bouncy, rubber ball. Still learning to walk, she toddles clumsily after it. She reaches down to pick it up, but when she tries to throw it, she falls backward. She plants her hands in the fragrant grass and heaves herself up to standing.

The ball rolls into the bushes, and she soon forgets

about it, stopping to allow the sun to warm her face. She squints down at the newly cut grass shimmering under her tiny shoes. Some flying insects buzz nearby. She is enjoying this beautiful day.

"Karina! Come here, baby!" her mother calls out to her. Her young mother appears on the patio near the back door. Because the sun is low in the sky, Karina can make out only the silhouette of her outstretched arms. She raises her own plump baby arms and begins waddling toward her. Her legs swish through the grass toward the concrete patio.

She is a moment away from being swept up into the safety of her mother's arms, when things suddenly grow dark and seem to slow down. As if in slow motion, Karina sees every minute detail of the moment her shoe catches on the crack in the concrete. She raises her foot to take the fateful step and is launched into the air. Her mother reaches for her and nearly catches her—or so it seems from her young mind's perspective.

And then, more quickly now, comes the rest: the concrete filling her view, her forehead slamming down on the gardening shears, the feeling of flesh being torn and blood splattering into her eyes, the panicked screams of her mother rushing toward her.

All this—the entire event—comes bursting forth

from the darkness that had concealed it. She opens her eyes and finally sees.

With her fall no longer hiding in her subconscious, Karina was overcome by shock and bewilderment. Now she could see how her fall, the sort of tumble many toddlers take while learning to walk, had robbed her of something essential, something she'd never been able to recover: an innocent trust in her surroundings. In her still-forming mind, her world—which until then had been benign and supportive—had turned suddenly, inexplicably violent and had attacked her without cause.

In an instant, she'd learned that the world was a dangerous place, that it would abuse her, slap her, cut her, make her bleed. Though still just a baby, she'd concluded that life was untrustworthy and that, in a flash, a beautiful, sunny day could be swept away in a tidal wave of pain.

This unlucky tumble, Karina now saw, had not only destroyed her belief in the safety and predictability of her world but had also lessened her place within it. In one disastrous moment, her forehead had been ravaged—her otherwise lovely features destined to be forever overshadowed by her scar.

Never again would adults gaze at her in admiration or comment on her beauty. Instead, she'd become an expert at detecting the revulsion in their eyes.

Over the years, she'd grow to detest mirrors, which were always there to remind her of her flaw.

Now that she could finally see her fall and the implications rippling toward her over the years, she was staggered by the weight of what had happened to her. The agony of flesh being ripped open lit up her forehead, and every cell shuddered from the shock. The taste of metal filled her mouth, and her vision blurred from the concussion. She crumpled to her knees, covered her face with her bloody hands, and began to wail. Powerful sobs took possession of her, as she shuddered and shook. Algernon stood a few feet away, his hands clasped solemnly before him.

After what seemed like a long time, the storm of tears began to dissipate, and Algernon stepped forward. He took a handkerchief from his pocket and held it out to her.

"Are you alright, my dear?" he asked, crouching down to place a hand on her back. She blinked up at him through her tears.

"I re-mem-ber," she gasped. To her surprise, she felt profoundly relieved.

"This was an important step," he said gravely. "Now you must rest."

Karina opened her mouth to protest but lacked the energy to do so. Her eyelids drooped, and she was barely able to nod in agreement. She collapsed onto the ground and let out one final sob.

With Algernon kneeling by her side, she closed her eyes and allowed unconsciousness to take her.

Chapter 10

Karina stands before the cement patio, staring at the cracked concrete and the inch and a half difference in height between the two halves. The gardening shears glint menacingly nearby.

She lifts her foot, just as she'd done all those years ago, but when she lowers it, the patio disappears. Instead, her foot lands on a concrete staircase suspended in another realm. She glances over her shoulder, but the backyard is gone. For as far as she can see around her, there's nothing but a dull grayness. It's just her and this floating staircase.

Stranded on the bottom step, she does the only thing she can: climb. As she peers into the yawning abyss around her, she tries not to imagine what would happen if she were to fall now.

She takes each step carefully and, as she approaches the top, begins to hear something in the distance. It's the sound of cheering reaching her from beyond the top step. Underneath the cheering there's a faint chant, but she's unable to make out the words. Nevertheless, she can feel the revelers' excitement and longs to join them.

When she reaches the top, a street leading to a leafy town square comes into view. An entire town's worth of people have gathered for an evening celebration. Karina glances back at the emptiness she's just left and decides she much prefers the square.

She makes her way up the street, past charming little shops with bright canvas awnings and carved wooden shingles. The quaint street lights and filigree iron benches seem like they're from another time.

When she nears the square, she sees the crowd clustered around a central bandstand. There, standing at attention, members of a marching band are dressed in shiny red-and-white uniforms. The drum major, in a black hat with a long white feather sticking out of it, holds his baton ready to move. The crowd cheers and claps, apparently waiting for them to play.

Karina spots an open area on one side of the square and heads in that direction to get a better view. She is making her way through the crowd, who are being held back by low barriers, when they suddenly part to allow a *gorgeous antique black convertible to pass. The striking vehicle, with its shiny chrome bumpers, perfectly polished mirrors, and windows that glitter in the setting sun, looks like the kind of vehicle a king or pope might ride in.*

As the car approaches, the townspeople suddenly turn to face her. Lined up four or five deep, they begin waving and smiling at her, and the cheering gets louder. Mothers strain against the barriers, while fathers hoist children onto their shoulders. A few people hold up pennants and signs, but she can't quite make out what's written on them.

The car stops directly in front of her, and a chauffeur in a black uniform and white gloves gets out to open the door. Karina questions him with a glance and again surveys the crowd, who continue to cheer for her as if she were some kind of celebrity. It's then that she realizes her name makes up part of their chant. Try as she might, she can't fathom what is going on or why these people would be cheering for her.

The chauffeur smiles politely and gestures for her to get in. She hesitates for a moment, then shrugs and allows him to help her onto the elevated backseat. The plush upholstery is delicious on her palms and the smell of opulence surrounds her. As she listens to the crowd chant her name, she feels the heat begin to rise in her cheeks.

She glances from face to beaming face and realizes that she recognizes some of these people. She sees her family, some kids from school, a few of her teachers— even the boy next door. She thinks she sees Gram and Mary Blair, too. It seems that nearly everyone she knows is here, along with many others she doesn't. Toward the back of the crowd, several people are holding up a six-foot long banner with her name on it. The townspeople continue to wave at her, and although she feels a little silly, she begins to wave back.

The car roars to life and starts slowly around the square. As it begins to move through the crowd, Karina hears the band strike up and looks back to see them fall in line behind her. It's a parade! But she hasn't done anything to deserve a parade. It has to be some kind of misunderstanding.

As the car inches forward, Karina scours the cheering crowd for clues as to what all the fuss could be about. Strangers young and old are jumping up and down and ecstatically shouting her name. Adults reach out to her, and children hold up sparklers. It doesn't make any sense at all.

Suddenly, there is a deafening explosion.

Fireworks unlike any Karina has ever seen fill the sky and rain down on the crowd, who "ooh" and "aah."

The bursts of color seem to come alive and dance in beautiful swirls and patterns. Some come together in the shapes of galaxies and star systems, while others form interlocking, three-dimensional patterns

The car stops, and the chauffeur gets out to open the door. Still stunned by all the adoration, Karina sits motionless. When the chauffeur beckons her out, she takes his hand and steps down onto a long red carpet with a white fringe. She looks down and thinks how strange her scuffed-up tennis shoes look against the luxurious carpet. This can't be right, she thinks. Someone has made a huge mistake. The crowd, the fireworks, the parade—it's all so surreal. She just stands there speechless.

Unsure what to do next, Karina glances back for another look at the car and catches a glimpse of her reflection in the window. As they've done a thousand times before, her eyes instinctively seek out her scar. This time, though, they do not return their quarry.

Bewildered, she approaches for a closer look and sees that her scar is no longer there. Her forehead is completely smooth, as if she'd never been injured at all.

She spins around to face the crowd, the breath vanished from her lungs. Before she has the chance to make sense what she's seen, a little girl with red hair falling in ringlets steps forward, her face glowing with excitement. Karina opens her mouth to ask her what is going on, but before she can speak, the girl thrusts an enormous bouquet of flowers into her hand and lowers her head in a curtsy.

Another burst of fireworks blankets the sky in shimmering color, and the band finishes with a flourish. The crowd goes crazy, letting out a great, rousing cheer. The fireworks reach a crescendo, and there's an explosion of light directly overhead. It's hypnotic, and she stares at the sky until the last sparks have faded. A reverent hush comes over the crowd.

Then, a brilliant white star appears on the horizon and begins to traverse the twilight sky. Though she does not understand the reason for this celebration, she decides to give in to it. She forgets her desire to know what is happening and embraces the moment. She doesn't know why she is here or what all these people are celebrating, but it feels good and that is enough. She closes her eyes and makes a wish.

"Karina." There was a hand on her shoulder. "Karina." She opened her eyes and felt the damp cave air on her skin. When she saw Algernon's worried face bent over hers, she realized that she was lying on the ground. He helped her get to her feet. She felt woozy, and for a moment, all she could do was stare at the grass. She let out a long sigh and looked up at him.

"Was that a dream?" she asked quietly.

"You might call it that," he answered. After a moment, he asked, "Is there anything else you'd like to know?" She remembered the way her forehead had looked in the dream and quickly reached up to feel for her wound. It was still there, fresh and burning to the touch.

"Ow," she said. "Yeah, I would like to know what happened to my head."

"You remembered. Remember?"

"Yeeees…?" said Karina, clearly unsatisfied with his answer. He gathered up his robes, took her by the arm, and led her toward the stream. There, he sat down on a high-backed wooden bench that bore a strong resemblance to a church pew and patted the spot next to him.

Eager for an explanation as to how her years-old injury could suddenly be bloody and raw, Karina sat down, her head throbbing. As she waited for him to speak, she wondered if she ought to be lying down.

"Karina, the universe—everything we see around us," he said, taking in the cave with a sweeping glance, "is made up of vibrations. The atoms and molecules that make up your body—and all other matter—are in a constant state of motion. At its most basic level, the universe is sound, wavelengths, vibration. 'In the beginning was the *word.*' In the beginning was sound, vibration."

Karina shifted uncomfortably on the hard bench.

"Your body," he said, touching her hand, "is held together by these vibrations. They are part of your essence, your soul, if you'd like. They're the reason you're able to inhabit your body." A thoughtful smile crossed his face. "When the soul experiences a trauma, the shock reverberates throughout the body. And the opposite is also true: When the body experiences a trauma, the shock reverberates throughout the soul. This is how the body and soul communicate, through the movement—the vibration —of emotion."

Karina started to nod, but the motion made her head hurt, so she stopped.

"Somewhere along the way—oh, a very long time ago—human beings began to turn away from their emotions." Algernon stared at the ground. "They stopped allowing certain ones to move, the inconvenient ones, the embarrassing ones—the ones they didn't like. And because of this, they lost something essential. They became just a little bit less human. Emotions are very important, you see. Without them, the body and soul cannot communicate."

He studied her face for signs of understanding.

"The problem occurs when something traumatic happens and the emotions aren't allowed to move. Instead of vibrating the way they're supposed to, they become stuck, frozen, unable to deliver their information. In cases of extreme pain or fear, for example, the mind may reject these emotions and deny them their place in the consciousness," he said. "When that happens, they cannot perform their essential role—to communicate."

He paused for a moment. When she was silent, he continued.

"Emotions that are not allowed to vibrate become frozen inside the body. It may seem as if they've disappeared or been forgotten, but they're still there, waiting for a time when they can do what they're designed to do. And when this happens, illness is the result."

Karina's face glimmered with recognition.

"Like repression?" she said.

"Exactly. The body and soul cannot heal from a trauma that has been repressed. Over time, people can become weighed down by an accumulation of repressed emotions." His face darkened. "They become heavy with sadness, anger, fear." He sighed. "And that, unfortunately, is the state in which most people live their lives. But you… you have been given a great gift. You have remembered your trauma. You can release the emotions surrounding it and finally heal."

Karina recalled the dream image of her smooth forehead and felt the spark of something unfamiliar. It was hope—hope that one day her scar might actually heal. They sat in silence for a moment.

"Now, I'm afraid it's time for you to return home, my dear," he said, standing. Karina got to her feet.

"Can I see the fish before I go?" she asked. Algernon hesitated but then saw the eagerness on her face.

"Of course," he said.

They approached the edge of the stream, and Karina peered into the water. She was about to ask where he was, when the fish leaped into the air, gave her a cheeky grin, and splashed back down. She knelt down at the water's edge.

"You splashed me!" she said, as he began to perform the backstroke.

"Beg your pardon, miss," he said. "Accidents do happen on occasion. And I see *you* have had an accident," he said, pointing his fin at her forehead.

"Yes, a long time ago," she said.

"A-ha!" he said. "And have you taken the time to release your emotional detritus?" He swished his tail.

"Emotional what?"

"You have suffered a terrible blow, *ma cherie*, have you not?" He stared at her intently. Karina thought his oddly human face was almost handsome and the dimples under his eyes quite adorable.

"Yes," she said, touching her wound.

"I see that it has gravely affected you. It affects you to this day."

"Yes."

"You humans are so funny! You don't realize that emotions are electric, rather like my cousin, the eel," he said, swimming in a slow circle. "If you're not careful, if you don't find the proper *outlet* for them," he said with a wink, "they can short-circuit. And do you know what happens then?"

Karina shook her head.

"You lose power!" He let out a short burst of laughter and rolled onto his back. As the sound echoed through the cave, Karina felt an odd sense of déjà vu come over her. She had the strange feeling that she knew this fish from somewhere, that she recognized his laugh.

"So, don't you think it's time you felt your pain, hmm?" he asked, resuming his backstroke.

"I must admit, it hurts a lot," she said. She wasn't sure whether she was more embarrassed by the blood or the pain.

"And it hurts even more," the fish said, placing a melodramatic fin on his chest, "in here. Am I correct?"

"Yeah," she said softly.

"Then you have your work cut out for you! You must take the time for this exceedingly important task: to feel. It's really quite simple:

> *"If you want to develop and grow*
> *There's something you simply must know*
> *In order to heal*
> *Your pain you must feel*
> *And let it rise up from below."*

He smiled, and Karina, utterly charmed by his dimples, couldn't help but smile back. She thought it absurd that a fish should have dimples, especially under his eyes. But everything about this fish—and this place— was absurd. He flicked his tail at her one last time and disappeared beneath the water.

Karina stood up and followed Algernon toward the bridge. She was fairly certain the assignment the fish had given her would not be an easy one.

"Algernon?" she asked, turning toward him.

"Yes?"

"I noticed some weird things after my last visit." She hesitated, but his intense gaze urged her on. "I felt like I knew what people were thinking, like I could read their minds or something. And some girls at school were way different to me."

"As you heal on ever-deeper levels, you will become aware of many things. There is much that the mind perceives and much more that it overlooks. Most people glimpse the deeper truth from time to time, but they simply don't recognize it. Perhaps you've noticed something out of the corner of your eye or gotten a strange feeling. You told yourself it was just your imagination. But it was the 'still, small voice'—the voice of your heart—trying to tell you something."

Karina nodded thoughtfully.

"But why would other people change?"

"Because the world is merely a reflection of your own energy. Change yourself and you will see your reflection change. As the wise Native American Chief Seattle once said, 'All things are bound together; all things connect.'"

Karina stared down at her sneakers and thought about the way they'd looked against the red carpet in her dream. She smiled and turned to leave.

Algernon called out to her.

"Remember, Karina, human beings have unfairly judged their emotions. Sadness, anger, fear, pain—they're all just messengers with important information to impart. They are your friends; heed their counsel."

Chapter 11

Before the first waft of creek bed air hit her face, Karina felt the agony of her injury well up inside her. She teetered from rock to rock until she reached the trail, where she fell to her knees and began to sob. Wave after wave of pain crashed through her as the tears came pouring out.

With every wrenching sob, she felt a little more relieved, as if she'd been holding her breath for a very long time and had finally decided to let go. The moment of her fall was so clear in her mind: the light afternoon breeze, the hazy sun in her eyes, her mother's voice calling her name. Details that had been tucked away in the crevasses of her mind were now crisp and vivid. And now that she was ready to accept them, the feelings that had been hidden from her all those years came roaring back.

She wailed and beat her fists against the hard, dry earth as the tears trickled off her nose. Her eyes became so swollen she could barely see, and the pain in her forehead grew until it encompassed her entire body. Hunched over on her hands and knees, she cried and watched as the blood and tears collected in a puddle on the ground.

After what seemed like a very long time, during which she cried uncontrollably, she finally sat back and rested her dirty hands on her knees. She blinked away the last of her tears and dried her eyes on her sleeve. Feeling that the flood of feelings was finally over, she got to her feet and continued home.

Every step required monumental effort, as if she were waking from a long sleep. But after a moment, the weakness began to subside, and she noticed the pain in her forehead had lessened. Although she had a headache from crying, she felt noticeably lighter, as if a weight she didn't even know she'd been carrying had been lifted. She became aware of a tingling sensation in the vicinity of her scar, where before there'd been only numbness and pain.

She also noticed the way the earth beneath her feet seemed to cushion and support her steps. It feels like a trampoline, she thought, as she bounced along the trail, noticing the plants and trees and sensing their aliveness.

By the time she stepped into the backyard, a sense of calm had taken root in her. At last she was done with the trauma of her long-ago fall. After all this time, it was finally over. The relief she felt at letting go was replaced by something new: a sense of certainty, of knowing.

A clearing had opened up in the forest of her thoughts, allowing her to comprehend the larger context of what had happened to her. Now she could see how distressed her parents had been by her accident, how they had tormented themselves for years over their failure to protect her, their little girl. She saw how their attempts to soothe her, though well intentioned, had actually helped the trauma to become stuck. Instead of allowing her natural instinct to cry, they had hushed her and begged her to stop. This had taught her the lesson that feelings are upsetting to others and therefore wrong.

She saw how her "recovery"—her body's attempt to accomplish the impossible task of healing without adequate time or space—had resulted in the formation of her scar. The scar had, in turn, affected her developing personality, convincing her that she was ugly and teaching her to be ashamed of her appearance. It had made her distrust people and fear their rejection.

The worst part, though, had been that it had convinced her that her feelings were unacceptable, embarrassing, and needed to be denied. And now that she had finally remembered her fall, she was sure that it would change her yet again.

Karina crossed the lawn in a trance. A butterfly flitted in a circle around her head, then flew off in the direction of the fence. The perfume from the night-blooming jasmine growing there captured her attention, so she headed toward it. As she approached a bough heavy with blooms and bent down to take in their sumptuous smell, it occurred to her that the sweet scent was Nature's way of soothing her.

When she'd had her fill, she stood up and noticed the neighbor boy watching her from the corner of his yard. She blanched, embarrassed to have been caught with her eyes so puffy and red. She told herself he probably couldn't see them from such a distance. When she met his gaze, though, she knew that he'd recognized her sadness. Had he heard her crying on the trail? She was too exhausted to care.

In the dimness, their eyes locked, and a strange bond was formed, each acknowledging the suffering of the other. When she smiled at him, he turned and disappeared out of view. She stood there for a moment, then made her way inside.

That evening up in her room, Karina found herself surrounded by the sounds of a typical Friday night: her brothers scuffling in their room, her mother washing dishes in the kitchen, her father on the phone with someone from work. And while these things stood in stark contrast to her experience in the cave—the one so

fundamentally different from the other—Karina realized
that she now felt a little less unhappy with her world. What
she'd learned in the cave gave her a new context for her
life, and she felt a dawning appreciation for what she'd
previously considered tedious. It seemed as though she'd
brought back with her a little of the cave's magic.

As she sat on her bed, Karina heard her brothers
tumble out into the hallway and chase each other down the
stairs. She waited until they were gone, then opened her
bedroom door and tiptoed out. When she reached the
bottom of the stairs, Henry ran up to greet her.

"Hey, Henry!" she cooed, bending down to pet
him. "What a good boy," she said, stroking his back.

He followed her into the storage room off the
kitchen, which doubled as her dad's office. She sat down
at his rickety roll-top desk and turned on the computer. She
had searched "reincarnation proof" and printed out a few
articles, when her father appeared in the doorway, the
phone in his hand.

"Hey, munchkin," he said, glancing at the printer.
"Whatcha doing?" He approached a stack of books and
newspapers in the corner.

"Dad?" she said.

"Yeah?" he answered, picking up a newspaper
from the stack.

"Do you believe in reincarnation?"

"Reincarnation?" He looked surprised. "Um…" He tucked the newspaper under his arm. "Well, let's just say I think it's pretty bizarre that we're born at all, so why not more than once?" he said, adding quickly, "But don't tell your mother I said that. It might freak her out." Karina nodded. "I'll tell you this, though…," he said to the phone in his hand, "…if I have to come back, I want a turn at being the boss. Those imbeciles."

"Honey, did you pack up that stuff for the Goodwill?" Karina's mom called out from the kitchen.

"On it!" He rolled his eyes at Karina. "I need a root beer. You want one?"

Chapter 12

The angle of the rays streaming through the blinds told Karina the sun had been up for hours. She snuggled under the covers, but there would be no going back to sleep. Instead, she lay there staring at the wall and listening to her brothers argue in the kitchen downstairs. Despite having been to the cave twice now, Karina was still struggling to accept that it was real.

She pulled on her bathrobe and joined her brothers at the table, where they were eating their Frosted Flakes. Her mom was in her nightgown wiping down the kitchen counter. Karina glanced between her brothers and her mother and had the overwhelming sense that she was a stranger in her own home.

"That's what I *said*," protested Jonah.

"Nuh-uh. You said 10 minutes."

"No, I didn't!"

"Yes, you did!" Max glanced up to see if their mom was listening. Seeing that she was miles away in thought, he attempted to kick Jonah under the table. Jonah anticipated this move, yanked his leg out of the way, and landed one of his own instead.

"Owwwwww!" said Max, clutching his shin.

"Boys!" Karina's mom rolled her head wearily toward them. "Oh, hi, Karina. Did you sleep well?"

"Yeah." Karina stood up, yawned, and approached her. "Mom, can you drop me off at Mary Blair's? She invited me to go over there before the sleepover."

"Sure, I have to go to the store anyway," she said, drying her hands on a towel. "Let me get dressed."

By the time her mother's car pulled up outside Mary Blair's house, it was early afternoon.

"Thanks, Mom," she said, hopping out.

"Jonah has a game. We should be home around 4:00," her mom said through the open window. The image of a sweaty, gleaming Parker scoring a goal, ripping off his shirt, and swinging it around his head flashed across Karina's mind.

"'Kay. See ya later." Karina climbed the steps to the front door and turned to wave conspicuously, hoping it would encourage her to drive away. It did.

She rang the doorbell, and Mary Blair's mother answered the door in stretchy black pants and a lacy, form-fitting top. Karina tried not to stare at her heavy makeup and overdone hair. Her droopy eyelids made her look like she needed a nap.

"Hey, darlin'!" she said, stepping aside to let Karina in. A waft of stale perfume hit her in the face.

"Hi, Ms. Fenner," said Karina, trying to smile. Ms. Fenner backed up toward an entryway table, where a cocktail glass was leaving a wet ring. She picked it up and took a sip.

"MB's up in her room. Go on up," she said, turning to saunter into the kitchen. Mary Blair had mentioned that her mom was a big drinker who sometimes got really mean after a night out. But all Karina ever saw was an overly friendly woman wearing clothes decades too young for her. Still, she was uncomfortable seeing her tipsy so early in the day.

"Thanks," said Karina, taking the stairs two at a time. At the top, she found the door to Mary Blair's room closed and rapped lightly on the only spot not covered in stickers and signs.

"Knock, knock!" she said.

"Who's there?" asked Mary Blair quietly.

"Archer," said Karina.

"Archer who?"

"Archer gonna let me in?" said Karina, bursting through the door. Mary Blair was sitting up in bed reading a magazine. She tossed it against the wall, where it tumbled into a pile of dirty laundry. One look at Mary Blair and Karina knew something was wrong. "Is everything okay?" she asked. Mary Blair sighed heavily, her chin quivering.

"Marco and I broke up."

"Aww, no! Really?" said Karina, as she sat down on the bed next to her. "What happened?"

"I don't know. He said he wants to 'keep his options open' or some shit like that." She looked up at the ceiling. "I told him to go to hell." She started crying, and Karina put her arm around her.

"I am so sorry! What a loser. You know you're better off without him, though, right?"

"Yeah. It's just… I really thought he was The One, y'know?" Mary Blair grabbed a tissue from a box on the nightstand next to her bed and blew her nose. Karina nodded silently, trying to hide her relief at hearing this news. Marco had already been arrested once for drunk driving. At least she wouldn't have to worry about her friend on the back of his motorcycle anymore.

"Anyone who would break up with *you* has got to be a total idiot."

"Thanks, dude. You're sweet," said Mary Blair.

"Are you ever going to see him again?"

"I doubt it. I threw a rock at him."

"What? Oh my God!" said Karina, grinning.

"I think it hurt, too, because I saw him limping after that." Mary Blair's smile dissolved into a sob. Karina shook her head and glanced toward the corner of the room, where a half-finished painting sat on an easel.

"What's that?" she asked.

"Well, I was *trying* to finish my art project before all this happened. I'm, like, totally boned. It's dogshit," said Mary Blair.

Karina stood up to examine the painting. It was a portrait of a woman from the 1940s with a mass of dark hair piled on top of her head. She was sitting in a high-backed chair wearing a red dress with sharp, pointy shoulders and a cinched-in waist. The general impression of the painting was of an uncomfortable woman in an uncomfortable chair. Mary Blair had finished the background, the chair, and the woman's dress but was struggling to paint her face. Where there should have been features, there were only a few vague smudges.

"I don't think so," Karina said. "It's just that... Is it supposed to be someone you know?"

"No. I mean, I kind of know what she's supposed to look like, but I just can't get it, y'know?" A disgusted look crossed her face, and she collapsed back onto the bed.

"It sucks."

"No, it doesn't," said Karina, bending over to peer closely at the canvas. For a long moment, she stared at the blank space where the woman's face ought to be. Slowly, it began to dawn on her who it was Mary Blair was trying to paint. She turned around and looked intently at her.

"Dude," said Karina, "it's you." For a moment, Mary Blair didn't move.

"What?" she said softly, sitting up. "Me?"

"Yeah, that's you… before," said Karina, pointing to the painting. "You just forgot what you looked like." He voice grew quiet. "You have to remember."

"Before? What are you talking about?" asked Mary Blair.

"That's you… before you were you," said Karina, shooting her an uncomfortable glance. She knew what she was saying sounded crazy, but before she could finish saying it, she saw the person Mary Blair had been clearly in her mind. Like a camera lens being brought into focus, Karina saw the general arc of the woman's life, along with a few major details.

In an earlier time, Karina saw, Mary Blair had been a beautiful and talented singer with dreams of hitting the big time. She'd pursued her ambitions to the exclusion of all other aspects of her life.

At one of her performances, she'd met and fallen in love with a gentle, loving man. After a whirlwind courtship, he'd asked her to marry him, expecting her to assume a traditional wifely role. But though they'd been deeply in love, she'd refused to give up her career, and their romance had ended. In fact, in that life she'd cut herself off from a string of people: friends, family, the child she'd given up for adoption. Her relentless quest for stardom had destroyed every last one of her relationships.

Despite her not-insignificant talents, in the end, the woman Mary Blair had been was able to achieve only modest, local renown. Her guilt had prevented her from advancing toward the goal she'd so cherished.

After sacrificing the love of her life and failing to advance in her career, she'd ended up desperate and alone, the residue of guilt and self-loathing caused by the choices she'd made blocking her from creative achievement. And now, here she was, in a new body, blocked again.

Karina then saw the end of her friend's life. With no family members or anyone else to care for her, she'd taken refuge in a homeless shelter, her career a distant memory. Suffering from alcoholism and tortured by regret over her unfulfilled dreams, she'd had a massive stroke at the age of 51. She'd passed away one blustery September morning, her only mourner the fiery maple tree growing outside her hospital window.

And now, here she was, back to atone for her sins, back for another chance at the love she'd refused, back in search of creative fulfillment—back for another try. Here she was, in a new body, living and breathing, again wrestling with her muse, the talent developed over countless lifetimes locked away inside her, just waiting to be set free.

"Do you remember?" asked Karina. Mary Blair's gaze traveled back and forth between Karina and the painting. She started to stand up but changed her mind and sat back down. She placed her hands over her eyes.

"No. I mean… It's weird," she said, shaking her hands as if to clear a space in front of her. "I can *imagine* what you are saying—I mean, it seems right—I just can't…" She froze for a moment, staring at the painting. She stood up and approached the canvas, placing her fingers on the empty space where the woman's cheek ought to have been.

She stood there for a long moment staring at her hand against the canvas.

"Oh my God," she said finally, touching her own face. "I think I do." She turned around to Karina, her eyes full of sadness and pain. The two girls hugged again and sat back down to look at the painting together.

Mary Blair began to recount some of the turning points in the life of the woman she'd been. She said she thought she'd been a teenager when the war began and that her father had been killed in Normandy. Her mother had struggled with alcoholism, too, and had died young of liver failure. The most indelible parts of her life, though—the pain she'd suffered, the lessons she'd learned—Karina had already seen.

Once the initial shock of remembering her former life had faded a bit, Mary Blair again started to cry.

"I think we knew each other then, too," she said, regret showing on her face. "I think you tried…," she said, the words catching in her throat, "to be my friend." Karina wrapped an arm around her.

"It's okay, Mary Blair," she said. "You don't have to be alone this time." Mary Blair was gazing mournfully into Karina's eyes, when she realized she had dripped tears onto her sleeve.

"Oh my God! I'm so sorry!" She grabbed a dirty shirt from her laundry pile and began dabbing at the spot. When Karina recoiled, they both started to laugh. Mary Blair looked embarrassed.

"It's okay," said Karina, smiling and placing a hand on her shoulder.

"Are you going to tell me how you know all of

this?" she asked, gesturing toward the painting. "Have you always known I was this horrible person?"

"No, no," said Karina. "I just realized it now—I guess because you were having so much trouble painting her face… I mean, *your* face… whatever."

"I think I can finish it now," said Mary Blair, turning to gaze at the painting. For a moment, it seemed as if she might cry again.

"Have you always been…," she asked, grasping at the air, "psychic?"

"No." Karina shrugged. "I don't know." She wasn't sure whether she was ready to tell her about the cave. "I can't explain it. But I think you're having trouble painting now because you still feel guilty about then." A panicked look swept across Mary Blair's face.

"Why? Did I do something terrible?" Before Karina could answer, Mary Blair's eyes narrowed. "Anyway, how do you know all of this?"

"I don't know. I just do," she answered. "I think you need to forgive yourself. When you were this woman…," said Karina, glancing at the painting, "…you hurt people—people you loved." Mary Blair struggled to hold back the tears.

"I don't think I liked myself very much—kind of like now." She grabbed another tissue off the nightstand.

"Yeah, but it's okay. You've got another chance now. You can do things differently this time," said Karina. Mary Blair wiped her eyes.

"How do you know this, seriously?" she asked. It was clear Mary Blair was not going to give up until she got an answer.

"I found this weird place," Karina said after a moment. "I'll just have to show you."

"Okay, but let's hit Borelli's on the way. I'm starving," said Mary Blair, jumping up to search for her overnight bag among the clutter in her closet.

Chapter 13

Outside, the girls glanced warily at the thunderclouds gathering in the sky. Mary Blair zipped up her hoodie, the black skull-and-crossbones pattern contrasting with her eyes, still red from crying. She heaved her overnight bag onto her shoulder, and they began the short walk to Borelli's. When they arrived, the parking lot was full, despite it being only five o'clock.

They caught the door as a group of drunk college boys came stumbling out. Karina giggled as a wide-eyed Mary Blair turned to her and mouthed "Oh my God!"

They stepped inside and were taken aback by the lively crowd. Parents chatted over pitchers of beer, while little kids ran back and forth. When Karina spotted a handful of boys in soccer uniforms, her stomach dropped.

"Oh, no! I forgot about the game," she whispered, closing her eyes. Mary Blair knew exactly what she meant: Parker would be here. Karina whipped on her sunglasses and darted toward a table in the corner. Mary Blair struggled to follow, her overnight bag banging against the backs of chairs as she made her way through the crowd.

"Wait!" she whisper-yelled, but Karina was already hunched over a table with her back toward the room. Mary Blair sat down opposite her.

"Well?" asked Karina impatiently.

"Looking… looking…," said Mary Blair, scanning the crowd over Karina's shoulder. In the center of the room, the players had pushed together several tables, w their parents sat scattered nearby. Then Mary Blair spotted Parker sitting at a table in the back with… Commander Bitch Avery!

"Oh… my… God," said Mary Blair quietly, a look of disgust on her face.

"What?" asked Karina, staring desperately at her friend, who was too stunned to speak. "Oh my God, if you don't tell me right now…" Mary Blair lowered her eyes like a doctor about to deliver a fatal diagnosis.

"Karina, it's going to be okay," she said, meeting her gaze. "He's with Avery." Karina sat bolt upright in her chair, tore off her sunglasses, and spun around. She scanned the room, her eyes locking on Parker, who was straddling a chair with his hand on Avery's knee. He was leering at her breasts, while she blushed and batted her eyes at him.

Bam! Just like that, Karina's heart exploded in a dark cloud of dust. For a moment, it felt as if her lungs had stopped working. The room began to wobble, and the air grew thick. She really, really wanted to cry, and even though she knew she needed to bawl and scream and flip over the table, she just sat there. The thought of this entire restaurant packed with people—including Parker and Avery—witnessing her heartbroken cries prevented her from taking a breath.

She pictured the fish's disappointment at this failure and slumped back in her chair. Only then did she see Mary Blair's mouth moving and realize that she had been speaking.

"…a girl like Avery. I mean, any guy who would fall for that ri*dic*ulous shit…," said Mary Blair, her nose in the air. "He must be a *super*-moron. I mean, she's not even that pretty," she said unconvincingly.

"It's okay. Thanks. I'm… I'll be okay," said Karina, pretending to dig through her purse in order to hide her face. Mary Blair gazed sadly at her.

"Of course you will," she said. Karina blinked a few times and decided to brave another look.

Parker had moved and was standing behind Avery, whispering into her ear and giving her a shoulder massage. Her eyes were closed and her arms hung limply by her sides. The relaxed smile on her face bordered on obscene. Mary Blair was about to say something encouraging, when the devastation that had shown on Karina's face suddenly condensed into cold, hard scrutiny.

Across the room, Avery was giggling at something Parker had said. He cocked back his head with a smug grin, and to Karina's amazement, his "other" face suddenly came into view.

For the first time since she'd laid eyes on this boy —since her heart had been ripped from her chest and placed in the palm of his careless hand—Karina saw his *real* face. And it was both frightening and repulsive. From across the crowded restaurant, she was able to peer past his handsome exterior and directly into his soul, to the person he was on the inside. And what she saw was truly ugly.

Written on this other face, Karina read Parker's narcissism and arrogant disregard for other people. She saw what a selfish, lazy liar he was and how he treated his mother with monstrous contempt. One look and she knew he had no real interest in Avery and was planning to dump her as soon as he'd finished with her.

This beautiful, blonde soccer star—who'd captured her heart, who'd monopolized her thoughts day in and day out for months, whose rejection had cut her so deeply—was, she now realized, a borderline sociopath.

Mary Blair, who'd been watching Karina undergo this inexplicable change of heart, sat there waiting for her to explain.

"Karina?"

"Oh my God," said Karina quietly, staring at Parker. Finally, she turned back to Mary Blair.

"What is it?" Instead of answering, though, Karina started to laugh. Mary Blair's confused smile was quickly replaced by an impatient frown. "What's wrong with you?" she asked, annoyed at being left out of the joke.

Mr. Borelli approached the table with their salads and cheese pizza.

"Evening, ladies," he said, unloading their plates from his tray.

"Hi, Mr. Borelli," said Mary Blair. Between giggles, Karina nodded her thanks. He shot her a mock-disapproving look, then placed two empty cups on the table. The girls grabbed them and headed toward the soda machine on the other side of the room.

"Oh my God, are you going to tell me what the F is going on?" Mary Blair asked in a whisper. Karina filled her cup with ice and turned to steal another look at Parker and Avery.

To the rest of the room, they were the perfect couple with their sun-kissed tans and model good looks.

But Karina saw them for the horrible people they really were. She turned back to Mary Blair, who was studying her with a combination of irritation and curiosity.

"He's a douche. I get it now," she said. When she was done filling her cup, she stepped aside to allow Mary Blair to fill hers.

"Well, I've been telling you that for months, girl!"

Back at the table, Mary Blair let out a long sigh and picked up a slice of pizza. "Why *all of a sudden* are you saying this?" she asked, taking a bite.

"I guess you could say I never actually *saw* him before," said Karina. "I know that doesn't make a lot of sense…" She took a sip of her drink.

"You got that right," grunted Mary Blair.

"I'd only ever seen him on the outside. But now…" she said, taking a thoughtful sip of her drink, "… now I can see the inside, too." Karina paused while Mary Blair chewed and considered this.

"It's good, right?" she asked. Mary Blair swallowed quickly.

"Hell yeah, it's good."

Chapter 14

The girls arrived at Karina's around dusk to find the house full. While her mother and father chatted and drank beer in front of the TV, Max and Jonah played in the backyard with Nate, a boy from the neighborhood. Karina grabbed a couple of diet sodas from the fridge, and the girls went out back. Karina handed a can to Mary Blair and popped the top on the other one.

They paused on the patio to sip and watch the boys, who were tossing around a Frisbee and ignoring the occasional drop of rain.

Nate threw the Frisbee to Max, then turned to grin at the girls. Max fumbled and then dropped it. He picked it up and threw it badly to Jonah.

"Do I have to beat your ass again, man?" asked Jonah, laughing and shaking his head as he jogged over to pick up the Frisbee.

"Useless," he said under his breath. Max blushed with embarrassment but did his best to shrug it off. Mary

Blair leaned in to Karina.

"Why is Jonah always such a dick to Max?" she asked. Karina turned to look at her little brother, whose throw to Nate had sent him scrambling into the bushes.

"It's a long story," said Karina, shrugging. "C'mon." She placed her can on a ledge next to the house, and Mary Blair did the same.

"Where're we going?" she asked.

"You'll see." Karina led her across the lawn, bisecting the boys' play area and prompting a round of curses and grumbles.

"Sorry, sorry," said Mary Blair, waving her hands.

They'd almost reached the far side, when Karina pulled up short, as if she'd suddenly remembered something. She spun on her heels toward Jonah and marched straight up to him.

A scowl instantly contorted his face, but when he saw the look in her eye, he was reminded of the handful of times she'd hauled off and beaten him to a pulp. He started to back up, and by the time she reached him, he'd retreated almost to the fence line.

She stopped and beckoned him with her finger like a cranky old grandmother. He took a step forward.

"What?" It was more a statement than a question. She knocked the Frisbee out of his hand. He looked shocked and indignant and was about to lunge at her, when her words stopped him.

"He thinks you're awesome, y'know," she said quietly. It was clear he had no idea what she was talking about. She cocked her head in Max's direction. "Max," she said. He snatched up the Frisbee, impatient for her to make her point. "He thinks you *rock*."

The anger drained from his face. He glanced over Karina's shoulder at his little brother, who stood there like an eager puppy waiting for a stick to be thrown. When he looked back at Karina, his eyes registered shame.

"Too bad you don't," she said with disgust, before continuing across the lawn.

With the rain now starting to pelt, Jonah lowered his head. He stared at the Frisbee in his hand and read the words printed there: "Hernandez Brothers Hardware— You're Part of Our Family."

"Over here," called Max.

Jonah looked up to see the expression on Max's face. He took careful aim with the Frisbee, and in the instant he let it go, understood what had been obvious to Karina, their parents, and everyone else they'd ever met: Max idolized him.

Jonah turned to gaze in the direction Karina had gone and saw her striding down the trail. Mary Blair was lagging behind, looking confused. For a moment, he wondered where they were going, then eyed the drizzle from above.

"Come on, guys," he said to Max and Nate.

While the boys retreated inside to get out of the rain, Karina and Mary Blair charged headlong into it. Twice Mary Blair asked Karina where they were going but got no answer.

By the time they reached the bottom of the trail, the ground was soaked.

"What the hell…?" Mary Blair called out. "Are you high? Dude, seriously?" She tightened the cord on her hoodie, but it did little to keep her dry. Karina, for her part, seemed almost unaware of the rain, which was being blown at an angle by the wind.

"Just come on," she called over her shoulder, as she slopped down to the creek bed. When she reached the spot where the cave door had been, she began tugging at the branches, which had grown up again to cover it. "Over here!" she called through the rising mist.

Mary Blair landed on the rocky creek bed and headed in the direction her friend had gone. When she rounded the embankment, she couldn't believe what she saw: a wet and determined Karina wrestling with a mass of roots and branches. Stunned, Mary Blair approached and was about to ask her what was going on, when Karina suddenly stepped back from the bank and gazed at her in stunned disbelief.

"It was here," she shouted over the downpour.

"What was?" asked Mary Blair. But instead of answering, Karina returned to groping at the damp leaves in rising panic.

Mary Blair watched her for a moment, then grabbed her by the sleeve and pulled her away from the bank. Karina stumbled back, the bottoms of her jeans soaked in mud, her fingernails jagged and black with dirt. The look in her eyes and the makeup running down her cheeks capped the general impression of a girl gone tragically insane.

"What the hell are you doing?" shouted Mary Blair, looking from Karina to the embankment. When Karina just stood there speechless, Mary Blair grabbed her by the wrist. "Come on!" she said, dragging her back toward the trail.

Half an hour later, up in Karina's room, the girls sat in silence. Karina was on the bed in her nightie, a towel wrapped around her head. She was picking the dirt from under her fingernails and looking embarrassed.

Mary Blair, who'd also showered and changed for bed, sat cross-legged on the chair. Confused and a little scared, she was waiting patiently for Karina to explain.

"What were you trying to show me?" she asked finally. Karina's brow furrowed, and she refused to meet her gaze.

"There was a cave…," she answered after a moment. Mary Blair waited for her to continue. In all the time they'd been friends, Karina had always been the sensible one. This episode had clearly troubled her.

"A cave?" she asked. Karina nodded and stared at the wall.

"There was a door… inside the hill," she said quietly. "And behind the door was a cave." Mary Blair shook her head vigorously for a moment and got up to join Karina on the bed.

"There was a room… I don't know, like a *room*… inside the hill. And there was a guy in there." Mary Blair's first thought was that her friend had had some sort of psychotic break. Afraid her face might betray her, she turned away and began examining her own fingernails.

"I wouldn't believe me, either, dude. But I *saw* it. There were plants and a stream and a bunch of other stuff. And there was this guy," she said. "He told me things." Mary Blair blinked her eyes, struggling to comprehend.

"Was it a dream?"

"No! I mean… no. I was wide awake. I'm sure of

it." Though Karina was adamant, her tone was tinged with doubt. Her face hardened, and she took a deep breath. "It was real. And when I left, I, like,… knew things. I *understood* things."

"Like previous lives?" asked Mary Blair.

"Yeah." The two girls went quiet for a moment.

"Karina, he didn't… *do* anything to you, did he?" asked Mary Blair, placing a hand on her back.

"No, no. It was nothing like that. We just talked. It was like he was waiting for me or something. I don't know." She sighed heavily and fell back on the bed. "I know it sounds crazy. That's why I wanted to show you."

"I guess… I mean, I believe you, Karina. I know you don't lie, I mean, not like some people," she said. Karina smiled meekly at the ceiling. "What do you think happened to it?"

"I don't know. But it was there yesterday. I saw it." Karina grabbed a pillow and hugged it. "Do you think I'm psycho?"

"No more than I am," said Mary Blair with a wry smile. "I mean, it's not like you saw a leprechaun or something." Her face turned suddenly mock-serious. "He wasn't a leprechaun, was he?"

"No," said Karina, cracking a smile.

"Thank God," said Mary Blair, feigning relief.

"You had me worried there."

Karina smiled, but she was more than a little shaken. Had she imagined the whole thing after all? She lay awake much of the night wondering.

Chapter 15

The sun had been up for hours when the girls began to stir. Mary Blair opened her eyes to see Karina wide awake and staring at the ceiling.

"Hey," she said, stifling a yawn.

"Hey," said Karina, still bothered by last night.

"Any plans for today?" asked Mary Blair.

"Lunch with my gram."

"Oh. That's cool." Mary Blair adjusted the pillow beneath her head. "I've got stuff to do anyway." Another lie, thought Karina.

Mary Blair was about to doze off again, when her eyes suddenly grew wide. She sat up and started sniffing the air. "Is that…?"

"Sure smells like it," answered Karina.

The girls got up, grabbed their robes, and hurried down to the kitchen. Mary Blair's mouth gaped when she saw the feast Karina's dad had laid out for them. There were piles of crispy bacon, stacks of fluffy pancakes, and a platter of eggs scrambled to perfection. In the center of the table, the house specialty: home fries with onions and peppers steaming in a cast-iron skillet.

"Yay!" said Mary Blair, clapping her hands and bobbing up and down. She grabbed a plate and grinned at Karina. In the kitchen, her dad stood sipping coffee in his wife's Wonder Woman apron.

"Orange juice?" he asked, opening the fridge and pulling out a carafe brimming with bright, pulpy juice.

"Absolutely!" said Mary Blair.

"Thanks, Dad. This looks amazing," said Karina, giving him a quick hug on her way to the table.

"You bet," he said. "I'm going to go check on Mom and the boys."

An hour later, the girls were sitting on the porch waiting for Mary Blair's mom to arrive. Mary Blair was glancing impatiently between the street and her overnight bag, while Karina had picked up a stick and was drawing in the dirt at her feet. She was trying in vain to replicate the fireworks she'd seen in her dream.

"Where the F is she? I swear, if she says she's going to be at a certain place at a certain time, you have to just automatically tack on half an hour," said Mary Blair. She jumped up, stomped out to the curb, and stared down the street.

"Dude, it's fine," said Karina with a wave of her stick. "She'll be here." Mary Blair returned, let out a sigh, and sat down on the step. Karina went back to tracing shapes in the dirt.

Mary Blair was just about to ask her what she was drawing, when they heard the screen door banged next door. It was the neighbor boy stepping out onto his front porch. The girls climbed to the top step to see if they could see over the hedge separating the two houses.

They could just glimpse the top of his head as he paused to stare dead-eyed at the house across the street. They followed his gaze and strained to see what he was looking at but saw nothing. They turned to exchange a wide-eyed glance.

"That guy is so weird," whispered Mary Blair. "My mom's friend said the school had to call the cops on him once. You know it's only a matter of time before he goes all Columbine." They watched as he muttered something to himself, then slumped down the porch steps and out of view.

"Yeah…," Karina said with a shrug. She just didn't feel right telling Mary Blair what she'd picked up about him.

"Finally," said Mary Blair, when her mother's dusty black Mustang pulled up. A wrist draped in bracelets hung sloppily out the window, long fake fingernails holding a cigarette.

"Hey, baby! How was it? D'you guys have fun?" she asked, taking a drag. Her gravelly voice was barely audible over the Guns N' Roses blaring through the car speakers. From the front, her hair was passably coiffed, but the back was a sweaty, matted-down mess.

Mary Blair tossed her bag onto the backseat, then turned to give Karina a kill-me-now look. She stepped back onto the sidewalk to give her a hug.

"Now I get to hear all about the 'great' guy she met last night, who probably, like, lives in his car," she whispered. Karina gave her a sympathetic look, and she climbed into the passenger seat.

Karina waved as the car pulled away and was heading inside when she heard the neighbor boy cough behind the hedge. Interacting with him was not something she'd ever considered, and there was certainly no reason to do so now. And yet, she felt something propelling her toward his side of the hedge, like the invisible hands of a mother urging a bashful child forward to greet a stranger. Though she had absolutely nothing to say to him, she decided to follow her instinct.

She took a deep breath and rounded the hedge.

She had taken only a few steps into the front yard

when the unsightly lawn choked with weeds and random junk strewn everywhere stopped her. Deciding that this was a bad idea after all, she had turned to leave, when she spotted the boy in the corner.

He was sitting cross-legged in the dirt in front of an old wooden doghouse. The dilapidated structure had once been red but was so badly weathered that only a few chips of paint remained. Next to him, propped up against the doghouse, was a beat-up acoustic guitar. He was staring at her feet.

"Oh, hey," she said, trying not to sound too awkward. In all the years her family had lived next door, Karina couldn't recall ever having spoken to him. A few months after they moved in, Karina's mom told her and her brothers to stay away from him. Mary Blair wasn't the only kid in town who was scared of him. And now that they were finally face to face, Karina had to admit that she, too, was a little afraid. He kept his eyes on the ground between them and said nothing.

"Whatcha doing?" she asked, approaching. When he looked away, Karina could feel the heaviness in the air around him.

"Nothing," he said quietly. She took another tentative step forward, wary of upsetting this lonely soul. When he dropped his head, she noticed a four-inch line in his scalp where the hair didn't grow. He's had a brain tumor, she thought, suddenly seeing a new context for his odd behavior.

"I didn't know you guys had a dog," she said in her sweetest voice. She sat down a few feet away. He eyed her suspiciously.

"We don't," he snapped. "I mean… We used to, but she died." As soon as he said this, Karina saw a picture of this boy's dog in her mind. She saw what a loyal companion she'd been and that he'd loved her with every shred of his being. This dog had been the center of his existence, giving him a reason to get up in the morning and something to look forward to when he got home.

Once he'd been released from the hospital, she'd been permitted to move inside and had taken up residence at the foot of his bed. In his otherwise chaotic and neglectful world, this dog had been something safe, warm, and reliable. And now that she was gone, whenever he felt empty, he would sit in front of her doghouse and remember the times she'd licked away his tears.

"Oh," said Karina, resisting the urge to give him a hug. The guitar again caught her eye, and she decided to change the subject. "Do you play?" she asked.

"No. It was my dad's. He left it when…" The boy got a pained look on his face and shook his head. Karina decided the subject of his dog was actually the safer one.

"What was your dog's name?" she asked.

"Franny," he said wistfully, "like *Franny and Zooey*, the book." For the first time the boy met her gaze. His hazel eyes overflowed with pain, anger, grief, and the memory of joy. "She was a really good dog." The word "dog" caught in his throat, and he looked away.

"I'm so sor—." But the boy jumped to his feet before she could finish. Suddenly and inexplicably angry, he glared at her. To reinforce that she was not a threat, Karina asked calmly, "Are you going to get another dog?"

"No," he spat, as if it were a ridiculous question. Though confused, Karina tried to stay calm.

"That's too bad," she said, getting to her feet, but he was already marching up the porch steps. He opened the screen door, stepped inside, and turned to give her a parting frown. Instead of slamming the screen door, though, as she expected, he closed it quietly behind him. He stared at her for a moment through the screen door, then disappeared inside.

"Oooookay," she said, reaching down to pluck a burr from her pant leg. As she headed back toward the street, she consoled herself with the thought that at least she'd let this boy know he could talk to her if he wanted to. By the time she'd reached her own front walk, her confusion at this strange rebuff had morphed into pity.

She was still trying to figure out what had upset him, when Gram's car pulled up.

"Grammy!" she called out.

Though she was only 63, Karina's grandmother looked years older, having lived, as she put it, an "interesting" life. After the death of her husband years earlier, she'd given up taking care of herself. She was 30 pounds overweight and had almost no muscle tone left in her arms. It was as if the flesh were slowly melting off her bones. When Grammy spotted Karina, she smiled, green eyes sparkling above sunken cheeks.

"Sweetpea!" she said, getting out of the car. She grabbed Karina by the shoulders and planted a kiss on her cheek. "What are you doing out here? Were you waiting for me?" She sounded surprised but happy.

"I guess so… yeah," she answered.

"You look beautiful, honey. So grown up!" Grammy gazed at her with pure adoration, something hardly anyone else ever did. "How is everything?"

"Good, good." She wondered if she ought to tell her grandmother about the cave, but then remembered the previous night's embarrassment. She put away the thought, but it was too late. Grammy had sensed her preoccupation.

"School alright?" she asked with a sideways tilt of her head.

"Sure, you know, the usual."

"Your mom told me you made the honor roll. That's fantastic, Karina!"

"Oh… yeah," said Karina, blushing.

"Come on, smartypants," said Grammy, tucking Karina affectionately under her arm. "Let's go see what your mom's up to."

Chapter 16

While the boys played Legend of Zelda upstairs, Karina and her parents sat in the family room debating where to go for lunch. When Karina heard them laughing instead of fighting, she gave herself a mental pat on the back.

"How about that crepe place?" asked Karina's mom, glancing at her husband.

"Ewww," said Karina.

"Well, alright then, missy. Where do you want to go?" she demanded.

Grammy emerged from the bathroom at the end of the hall looking pale and distracted. Before entering the room, she dropped whatever was bothering her and plastered on a smile. But Karina had seen this and was instantly worried.

Grammy crossed the room and sat down carefully in the easy chair next to the couch. Her face was ashen, and she seemed to be moving very slowly. She looks so old, thought Karina.

"How about that new Chinese place?" asked Karina, her eyes glued to Grammy. Grammy nodded excitedly and winked at her.

"I could go for that," said Karina's mom, glancing at her husband.

"Chinese it is, then," said Karina's dad. He stood up, grabbed his jacket from the back of the couch, and began fishing around in the pockets. Everyone except Grammy stood up.

"Honey, have you seen my keys?" asked Karina's dad. "I could've sworn…"

"I saw them on the dresser last night." Karina's mom stared at him for a moment, then turned to march upstairs. "Did you leave them in your pants?" she asked, as they trudged up the stairs together.

Karina approached Grammy and offered her a hand. She took it but made no effort to stand.

"Sit down a minute, Karina," she said. Her face had lost its pretend cheerfulness. Karina felt a slow wave of dread crash down on her.

"Okay," she said, sitting down on the ottoman in front of Grammy's chair. Grammy inched forward in her seat and cupped Karina's hand carefully in both of hers. Karina smiled weakly at it and held her breath as tiny beads of sweat sprang up on the back of her neck. She was absolutely sure she did not want to hear what her grandmother was about to say.

"Karina, there's something I have to tell you." She took a deep breath, then let it out. "I saw Dr. Wilson last week. That stomach problem I told you about… I'm afraid it's quite bad." Karina's eyes grew wild.

"Okay, so, what did he tell you? There's got to be something they can do. Mom and Dad can…" Karina gestured frantically toward the stairs.

"Karina… Sweetpea…," said Grammy softly, a strange, sad smile showing on her face. Karina bit down, willing herself not to jump up and run around the room screaming at the top of her lungs. Her heart was beating in her ears, and she could feel a sob crawling up her throat.

"You and me are a lot alike. Ever since you were a baby, I knew you had my… sense. Do you know what I'm talking about?" Grammy asked, looking squarely at her.

"You…? Do you mean you can… tell things about people?" asked Karina, hesitant to say it out loud.

"It's nothing to be afraid of," she said, closing her eyes for a moment. "It can be jarring when it first comes on, I know. When it happened to me, I thought maybe I'd gone to one too many Grateful Dead concerts or something." She laughed. "Your great-grandmother had it, too." Karina looked surprised.

"Does Mom?" she asked.

"Oh, no." She shook her head and gave Karina a sideways smile. "Your mother's much too logical. But, I don't know, sometimes she seems to know things she's not supposed to. She's not like you and me though. We're different, don't you think?"

Karina tried to smile.

"The important thing to remember…" said Grammy, as she lovingly cradled Karina's hand, "is that it's there to help you. Just think of it as your best friend, something you can always count on. Sometimes it'll seem far away, sometimes it'll be shouting right in your ear. But always, *always* listen to that voice." Grammy's words were like a gentle caress. "Because it'll never lie to you or send you down the wrong path. Okay?"

Karina nodded. Grammy looked at her for a long moment, then continued.

"Anyway, I wanted to tell you about the dream I had a couple of nights ago." She cocked her head to one side and seemed suddenly weary. Karina held her breath. She wanted to shout NO! NO! NO! but instead sat perfectly still.

"It was so real. I was lying in a little rowboat tied to the end of a dock. I could see all the clouds in the sky, and I could hear the water splashing up against the side of the boat as it rocked back and forth."

Karina struggled to take a breath.

"I was really tired, and everything seemed to be happening in slow motion. The boat was rocking so slowly." Her brow furrowed for a moment. "After a while, I got up and went onto the dock, and at the end of the dock was a forest. And even though it was dark in there, I could hear the birds chirping, and it seemed… nice, peaceful… like somewhere I'd like to go."

Grammy glanced at Karina to see if she was following.

"Other than the lake, the forest was the only place to go. And I knew that if I went in there, I would die." She paused before continuing. "I could either stay in the boat or go into the forest. And I chose the forest." Karina looked nauseous but kept her eyes on Grammy.

"Honey, I'm going to die," Grammy said, letting go of her hand and leaning back against the chair. "Soon."

Karina couldn't control herself anymore. She shot to her feet and began desperately pacing the room as if looking for an escape. At a loss for what to do but still in a panic, she sat back down and began to sob.

"Why? Are you sure?" she pleaded. "I can't lose you. You're the only one who gets me." Karina fell onto Grammy's knee and began to wail quietly. The old woman patted her head, and they cried together for a moment. When Karina sat up again, her eyes were streaming with tears. "Please don't leave me, Gram."

Grammy picked up a box of tissues from the table next to her, pulled one out, and handed the box to Karina, who tugged on it until she had four or five.

"It's okay, Karina. Let it go," she said, watching sadly as Karina wept. When Karina paused to catch her breath, she noticed Grammy gazing at her with an uneasy blend of guilt and affection.

"I love you so much, Karina."

"I love you, too, Grammy," she said, raking the tissues across her cheeks. "Do Mom and Dad know?"

"Well, I didn't tell them about my dream, if that's what you mean," she said. "It wouldn't have meant anything to them anyway. But they know I'm terminal," she said to the tissue in her hand.

At the sound of this word, Karina choked back another sob.

"When?" asked Karina finally, her voice pinched.

"I don't know exactly. Could be days, could be weeks," said Grammy shrugging. "But it's okay." Beneath her sadness was a steadfast resignation. "I've lived a good life. It's time for me to let go of this old body and move on to something new."

As Grammy gazed at her, Karina saw the profound affection in her eyes. Although it was clear she'd been suffering for some time, it seemed as if the only thing she cared about was how Karina was taking the news.

Her head pounded, and she felt like throwing up. The thought of losing her beloved Gram was a devastating punch in the gut. She wondered how many more times she would be able to see her, to talk to her, to hold her hand. Just as the tears began to well up again, her mother appeared at the top of the stairs.

"Could they be in the car?" she asked, trying not to sound annoyed.

Karina jumped up and headed toward the bathroom. Before she was out of reach, Grammy grabbed her by the wrist and pressed a finger to her lips. Karina nodded sadly and made it to the bathroom just as her mother reached the bottom step.

"They're right here, John!"

As she stood at the sink splashing cold water on her face, Karina could hear her mother jingling the keys in the hallway.

Chapter 17

Lunch was surreal for Karina. The conversation she'd had with Grammy gave even the minutest details of the afternoon a morbid significance. Was this the last time Grammy would walk down this street, the last time she'd eat a fortune cookie? Karina had to keep reminding herself that the woman who always seemed to understand her when nobody else could was still here. She was here right now, at this table, breathing, laughing, smiling—alive. It was the only thing that got her through the meal.

Later that afternoon, the Morgans' faded green Subaru had barely rolled to a stop in the driveway, when the boys jumped out and ran inside to play Zelda. The game that had assumed such a monumental place in her brothers' lives struck Karina as an insulting triviality. In fact, everything about the day seemed trivial under the circumstances.

Though she was disgusted by their obsession with this stupid game, Karina reminded herself that they had no way of knowing how sick Grammy was. Still, she couldn't help but wonder if knowing would have made any difference at all.

Karina's dad went inside, while Grammy, Karina, and her mother paused on the front porch to say goodbye. A moment later, he returned carrying an overstuffed box marked "Goodwill."

"Did you get the bags from the kitchen?" asked Karina's mom.

"Bags? Uh, no," he said. "Karina, could you put this on the backseat for me?" Karina took the box and went over to the car. As she heaved it onto the backseat, a book fell out and landed at her feet. She picked it up and read the title: *Teach Yourself to Play Guitar*.

"Hey, Mom, can I have this?" she asked, holding up the book for her mother to see.

"Sure, I guess." She shrugged and went back to talking to Grammy. Karina's dad returned with two garbage bags and tossed them on top of the box. He kissed Grammy, got in the car, and backed out.

"Wanna come in for some coffee, Mom?" asked Karina's mother.

"Oh, thanks, but I'd better be going. I've got some things to do." She gave Karina a wink.

"Okay. See you Thursday, then." Karina's mom

gave Grammy a kiss and turned to go in.

As her mom disappeared inside the house, Karina caught Grammy's gaze lingering on the door as it closed behind her. She wondered how much differently this goodbye might have gone if her mother knew what she and Grammy did—that it might very well be their last.

Karina laid the book on the porch step and turned to face Grammy. She dug deep for something to say, but all she could do was bite her bottom lip in a vain attempt to stop it from quivering.

Grammy stepped forward and wrapped her arms around Karina with as wide a hug as she could manage. Karina clung desperately to her, refusing to let go, though she knew that this embrace had to end—if not now, then next week, if not next week, then next month. To deny that her illness, which had been getting steadily worse, would one day take her life was to deny that even the brightest of days will end in darkness. It was simply a matter of time.

Grammy pulled away, and the two looked deeply into each other's eyes. Karina saw that underneath a thick layer of grief at having to say goodbye to her family, Grammy was resolute. Death did not scare her. The creases at the corners of her eyes, the limp flesh of her arms, and the disease that was stealing a little bit of her strength each day could not hide the woman she was inside, the vibrant young woman who had always been Grammy—and always would be.

I will see you again, thought Karina. To her surprise, Grammy nodded, almost as if she'd heard.

"My sweet baby," said Grammy, gently touching her cheek. "It's going to be okay. Come." Grammy took Karina's elbow, hugging it to her, and led her out to the sidewalk. They made their way down the street, Grammy smiling peacefully at the pavement as they strolled along. Searching for words to match her feelings but finding none, Karina allowed Grammy to lead her in a silent procession.

When they were halfway down the block, Grammy stopped and turned to her. She reached into the pocket of her cardigan, pulled out an embroidered handkerchief, and unwrapped it. Inside was a gold chain holding a pendant in the shape of a shooting star. A tiny diamond sparkled in the center. She placed it carefully in Karina's hand.

"I want you to have this. My mother gave it to me when I was a little girl." Karina blinked away the tears and struggled to focus on the pendant. "She brought it back from a trip she and my dad took to Italy." Grammy gazed wistfully into the distance, as if seeing a vision of her mother before her. "Your great-grandma had the most beautiful teal-blue eyes you've ever seen," she said, gently lifting Karina's chin. "And with those eyes, she could say things that only I could understand."

Just then, a breeze blew up, and Grammy shivered a little. She pulled her cardigan around her and continued down the sidewalk, Karina close at her hip.

"Her unusual talent—it freaked my father out some. You should know that it'll frighten some folks. His parents were very religious, you see, and brought him up to be afraid of stuff like that—stuff they didn't understand. I will say, though, he never seemed to mind her 'skills' when they were looking for a parking space at the mall." A slow laugh rolled through her. "She was an amazing woman." Karina sniffed and tried to breathe.

"Though I may soon… go away… physically, I will still be able to hear you if you ever want to talk to me. Okay, Karina?"

At the sound of this, Karina felt a burning rage flare up inside her. She desperately wanted to fall to her knees in a slobbering pile, break her fists on the sidewalk, and scream the most vile obscenities at God—or whoever was up there. Instead, she smiled weakly.

"You will *always* be my Starina. Just remember that." Karina nodded.

They hugged each other tightly, and the breeze

whipped around them. When Karina blew her nose on the handkerchief, Grammy gave her a sideways look.

Karina managed a brief chuckle, and they began the slow walk back to the house, their steps in perfect sync. Though they didn't speak, Karina knew that Grammy was communicating with her, practicing being there and not being there so Karina could get used to the idea. Each was intent on soaking up as much of the other as possible in the time they had left.

When they reached the car, Grammy turned to her.

"I've got to go, Sweetpea. I love you." They hugged again, and Grammy planted kisses on both of Karina's cheeks. Her heart thumped against her rib cage as Grammy got into her car and backed out. She watched her grandmother's car turn the corner out of view and wondered if she'd ever find anyone else to love her as much as Grammy did.

As she stood there wishing she could be with her grandmother forever, she gradually became aware of a pain in the center of her palm. She glanced down and realized she'd been clutching the pendant so tightly, it had left a mark in her flesh.

Karina dabbed her swollen eyes with the handkerchief and examined the pendant more closely. She turned it over in her hands, admiring its simple elegance and vowing to treasure it forever. She imagined Grammy's little-girl happiness at receiving such a gift and the smile it must have brought to her face. Then she remembered the dream she'd had in the cave and the star that had shot across the sky. She kissed the pendant, unclasped the chain, and placed it around her neck.

The sound of the screen door banging next door announced the neighbor boy's presence. Karina wiped her nose, tucked the handkerchief into her pocket, and grabbed the guitar book off the porch.

She crept around the hedge, where she found him sitting in his spot in front of the doghouse.

"Hi, again," she said, hoping it wasn't too obvious she'd been crying.

"Hi, again," he parroted. He did not meet her gaze but kept his eyes on the book instead.

"We were cleaning out the garage and I found this. I thought you might want it." She held it out to him.

After what seemed like an eternity of glancing between the book and the dirt at his feet, the boy finally took it.

"Thank you," he said, flashing a strained grin. Karina smiled back.

She stood there for a moment wondering if she should engage him further but decided against it. She turned to leave and, as she rounded the hedge, glanced back to see him flipping through the book.

Chapter 18

Karina slipped into her room without anyone noticing the pendant or her puffy, red eyes. She locked the door and set her alarm clock to play the sound of waves crashing on the beach. She'd decided to put Algernon's theories to the test and try letting her emotions flow through her instead of always stifling or ignoring them.

She stretched out on her stomach, put her face in her pillow, and set about bawling. After all, she thought, if I feel like crying in the privacy of my own room, who's to say that I can't?

When she finally rolled onto her back twenty minutes later, she was tired, hot, and thirsty. And oddly calm. She reached up to turn off the alarm clock.

She was tired and her eyes stung, but she also felt relaxed and alert. As her heartbeat and breathing returned to normal, she began to notice things about her surroundings she'd missed before. It was as if she'd suddenly become more aware of what had been there all along. It feels like waking up, she thought. As she lay there stretched out on the bed, she was able to perceive a whole bunch of new things, such as the pattern of the comforter's weave against her skin.

She realized that what she had thought of as a quiet room was actually teeming with sounds—the faraway gush of water as someone flushed the toilet downstairs, the barking of a dog at the end of the block, the buzzing of a tiny gnat at the window. Things that were usually on the edges of her awareness were suddenly front and center, clamoring for her attention.

Even the air was full of information—she thought she could smell perfume from the bottle across the room. For a few minutes, Karina listened and smelled and felt just a little bit more alive.

She sat up and grabbed a tissue from the box on her bedside table. She dabbed her eyes and lay down again, welcoming the new sensations. She became aware of her own breath and noticed its rhythm. Inside her chest, she felt her heart beating with reassuring regularity.

As the wave of pain and sadness subsided, she did what Grammy and Algernon had told her to do and tuned in to the quiet voice inside her. It spoke to her simply and directly: "Good. Now rest." She was so startled to hear an actual voice inside her head that her whole body jerked, causing the bed to jiggle.

Right away, she knew that this was not the do-this-do-that-what-if-something-terrible-happens-and-by-the-way-you-suck voice of her mind in its usual state. This was different. It was a clear, calm, loving voice that sounded like her own voice, except that it spoke *to* her rather than *for* her. Though it was inside her head—just like the normal voice she heard when she had a thought—this voice seemed to come from somewhere else, somewhere outside her finite body and mind. Or deep with in it, she wasn't sure which.

It had an unquestionable authority to it—and it was kind.

Of course, she hadn't expected to hear an actual voice inside her head—one that she had not initiated herself. But then she remembered Grammy's words. She got up to flip off the light and close the blinds. She lay back down and breathed deeply, focusing her attention on the plastic stars glowing on the ceiling above her head. Within a few minutes, several new memories had bobbed to the surface.

She saw herself with Grammy in what looked like pioneer times. They had lived in a wooden cabin with a wooden floor and had slept under animal pelts. They had grown dangerously thin in winter, and in warmer months, had spent most of their time outside. And while it had been a tough existence—she shivered at the memory of the ferocious winters—they'd shared many happy times together. In that life, Grammy had been her older sister and had raised her after their mother died of fever.

In another flash, Karina saw herself sitting under a tree overlooking a field of flowers. A million purple peonies swayed in the sunlight, as she and Grammy sang beautiful harmony together. Grammy had been her favorite childhood friend then, and they had lived in the same small village. They seemed to be of the privileged class, as they wore fine, starched-linen dresses and ribbons of pastel satin in their hair. Karina recalled laughing and singing and telling stories on a breezy summer day.

Karina knew she wasn't just imagining these times with her grandma. They felt distinctly like memories. As she lay there breathing and remembering, she came to believe that she and Grammy had been together many times before. And the only logical conclusion, she thought, was that they would be together in the future, too. The idea was tremendously comforting and took some of the sting out of the prospect of losing her now.

When she finally sat up, Karina felt lighter, the weight of sadness vanished from her chest. She was now sure that, although Grammy would soon be leaving her, the separation would actually be only temporary.

As she stood up, she caught sight of herself in the mirror above her dresser. For a moment, she stared in stunned confusion at her reflection. There was something about the girl staring back at her that just wasn't right.

She approached for a closer look, slowly crossing the darkened room with her eyes locked on the image reflected in the glass. When she was about a foot from the mirror, she stopped. Her mouth fell open and a quiet yelp came out. Against any semblance of reason, on this otherwise perfectly ordinary day, in the stillness of her unremarkable bedroom, a miracle had just occurred.

Her scar was gone!

Karina's hand flew to the spot where it had been. She knew this three-inch piece of flesh all too well, had spent countless hours obsessing over it, covering it up, wishing it weren't there.

But as she stood there staring into the mirror, she was unable to detect even the slightest bump or discoloration. She was certain it had been there earlier, had seen it in the bathroom mirror. But somehow, in the space of an hour, all evidence of her injury had vanished. Her fingers plied the place where, for as long as she could remember, her scar had frowned back at her.

She rushed to flip on the light and leaned in to

examine her forehead from every angle. But there was nothing there except clear, virgin skin.

Still refusing to believe her eyes, Karina began stretching and twisting the skin between her fingers, searching for a pucker, an unevenness, any trace of the wound that had tormented her for so long.

But there was nothing.

She strained to understand how this could have happened, but elation quickly took over, negating any desire to understand. Her scar had finally healed—that was all she knew.

"It's gone! I can't believe it!" she squealed to the empty room. She started jumping up and down and laughing and crying all at once. She dashed toward the door but remembered it was locked. She fumbled with the lock and, when she finally got the door open, swung it so violently it banged against the opposite wall.

"Mom! Mom!" she yelled, running down the hall.

Chapter 19

Later that evening, the rush of excitement and joy now faded a bit, Karina found herself alone in the backyard. A peaceful calm enveloped her as she wandered out into the middle of the lawn. The cool air licked at her arms, and she again tuned in to the world around her. A chorus of crickets and the gentle rasping of trees filled her ears.

Along the horizon, the outline of storm clouds receded into the distance. She threw back her head and breathed in the night, and in a way she never had before, sensed the life force coursing through her limbs.

The stars beamed down on her as she traced the Milky Way with her finger. The celestial panorama seemed infinitely far away and yet somehow just out of reach. She closed her eyes and smiled at the thought that no one would ever be able to call her Scarina again. Through some unknowable mechanism of the universe, some astonishing act of grace, she had been healed. Or perhaps she had healed herself, she wasn't sure which. She didn't know how it had happened, and she didn't care. All she knew was that she had regained something she'd thought irretrievable. She had been brought back to herself, back to the person she'd been before her fall.

She was restored.

The grass, the sky, the stars—everything was exactly as it should be. And so was Karina. Her euphoria made her feel like twirling, so she stuck out her arms and started spinning, watching as the sky rotated above her. When she felt the pendant begin to fly up on its chain, she stopped to admire it.

"Starina," she said to the pendant as she tucked it into her shirt. She couldn't remember a single time in her life when she'd been as happy as she was at this very moment. She felt almost transcendent, as if she might leave her body any minute and fly up to join the stars. The sound of a nocturnal creature scurrying among the leaves brought her back to her surroundings.

"Find your cave." The voice was like an invisible twin speaking directly into her ear. With perfect trust in what she now knew was the voice of her own heart, the part of her that was beyond pain, scars—and yes—even death, Karina immediately headed toward the trail.

She was still blushing with happiness when she landed on the creek bed a few minutes later. She recalled the last time she'd been here, when she'd been unable to find the door, and knew even before reaching for it that the handle would be there.

Once again, the door to the cave had been transformed. Now it held a large silver handle with baroque spirals forming the letter K. The door itself was covered with panels made from mother of pearl and inlaid with moonstones in a pattern that reminded her of the stars on her bedroom ceiling. The door was so lavish and beautiful, that despite her eagerness to enter, she paused for a moment to admire it.

When she finally stepped into the brightness of the tunnel, she was overwhelmed by its appearance. Lined from floor to ceiling with brilliant white marble, the walls were decorated with sculpted niches holding sparkling crystal vases filled with fragrant bouquets. The tunnel was so gorgeous, Karina couldn't wait to see what the cave would look like. As she neared the opening, she heard a sound ringing from its depths. She stopped to listen.

"Ha, ha, ha, hee!" Her grandmother's joyful laugh was unmistakable.

"Grammy!" Karina bolted toward the sound and had almost made it across the bridge when she was stopped in her tracks by the shimmering spectrum of light. She stopped to allow her eyes to adjust, and when they had, she beheld sheets of sparkling gems draped across the ceiling and colorful jewels glittering from every corner.

The flowers and trees were now made of fine-cut glass, and the grass was once again clear. Instead of ice, though, the grass was now made of sparkling crystal. A warm glow filled the cave, shedding exquisite rainbows in every direction.

The magnificent sight took Karina's breath away.

"Grammy?" Karina repeated, stepping off the bridge and into the cave.

"Grammy isn't here, I'm afraid," said a voice next to her. She turned to see Algernon, who was once again transformed.

Here stood a decidedly young man wearing a loose garment of pale, shimmering fabric with long flowing sleeves that nearly covered his hands. It reminded Karina of the kind of dress an angel might wear. His dark beard had been replaced by a thin scruff that barely covered his chin. He approached and offered her his hand.

"She will be near you when you need her. But you already knew that, didn't you?" As he helped her off the bridge, his smile bordered on laughter.

"What is it?" she asked.

"Come, come," he said and led her to the center of the cave. There, an object in the shape of a large chair was draped in a cloak of fine purple silk. He paused dramatically before whipping it away to reveal a shining crystal throne studded with thousands of diamonds. Karina gasped. She stepped forward to touch the armrest, which was ornately carved with creeping rose vines. The play of light off the clear crystal was spellbinding.

On the seat was a crushed velvet cushion of the deepest violet. A matching crystal footstool stood nearby.

"Holy crap! Are these real?" Karina asked, pointing to the diamonds.

"Of course, my dear! Everything here is real." He spun her around so she could sit.

"Me? Um, okay," said Karina. She sat down carefully, afraid to damage this priceless piece of furniture. Algernon sat down on the footstool in front of her. His face, now supple and smooth, was glowing.

"How are you, Karina?" he asked.

"Great!" she said.

"Wonderful. As you can see, the cave has also improved," he said. She ran her hand along the armrest and wondered how something made of crystal could be so comfortable. "You must be doing very well, indeed," he said, smiling.

Karina was overcome by a sudden desire to embrace him, so she did. For a moment, he seemed startled but then enthusiastically returned the hug.

"Thank you," she said.

Karina sat back on the throne and enjoyed the feeling of the velvet against her skin. She closed her eyes and allowed a wave of delight to wash over her. She marveled at the changes she'd undergone since she'd first stumbled upon the cave. And yet, despite her contentment, a stubborn curiosity bubbled up inside her. There were still so many things she wanted to know.

"Algernon?" she said, opening her eyes.

"Yes?"

"I was wondering… Is it okay if I ask you some more questions?"

"Of course," he said. She looked up at him, a crease in her brow.

"Why was the cave gone when I tried to show my friend?"

"This cave is yours and yours alone, Karina. Everyone must find the entrance to his or her own sacred space." His voice was patient and kind. "There are people, teachers, who can point the way and offer advice and encouragement, but the journey must be taken alone."

"Does everyone have a place like this?" she asked.

"Everyone," he said unequivocally. "Although most people—oh, I'm afraid to say, the vast majority—

never even look for it." The light in his eyes dimmed. "And so it remains hidden, which is most unfortunate, for them and for the world. Every time someone does what you have done—go in search of inner treasure, the hidden realm within each of us—a drop of love is added to the world. And although it be only a single drop, it causes a ripple that spreads out to the entire world. It's so powerful, it can even affect strangers. And when that happens...," he said, holding his thumb and index finger an inch apart, "... the world gets a tiny bit better. You see, the universe exists in a kind of ether, a soup. And the main ingredient of that soup is love."

"Love soup?" asked Karina.

"Yes." He nodded. "The universe could not exist without this soup, because it's love that holds everything together. It holds the molecules of your body together. It holds this cave together. It holds the galaxies together. Without it, human beings could not exist." Karina looked thoughtful. "When we're born, we forget this love. We go away from it, only to begin the slow journey back. It's the very reason we *are* born, so that we may forget."

"But why do we have to forget?" she asked.

"Because the world is like a playground, where souls come to play and learn. Sometimes you have a bad experience—you stumble and fall. You end up with cuts and bruises and go home crying."

"Other times, you swing high and have a wonderful time. At those times, it can feel as if the world is one big circus and you're the star performer. And whether you realize it or not, your experience on the playground is created entirely by you, by your beliefs and actions—by your karma. The reason life can seem so confusing, so frustrating, is that we don't remember *how* we created it, because we created much of it before we were born."

Karina stood up and stepped away from the throne. Algernon followed.

"Why do we have to get hurt, though?" she asked.

"Because when human beings forget where they've come from, they forget a lot of other things along with it. Many a bored housewife has talents she can't even imagine. She *has been* the brain surgeon, the concert pianist, the world leader, the fighter pilot. She just can't remember it. But that part of her is still there, buried deep inside her. It's just sleeping, for want of a better word."

Karina, who had been staring thoughtfully at the crystalline blades of grass, met his gaze. He nodded at her silent demand for an answer.

"For reasons having to do with human psychology and physiology, pain is one of the most effective…," he said, searching for the right word, "…alarm clocks there is. Nothing wakes one up quite like a good bump on the head." He gave her a sad smile.

"The lessons pain has to teach us are not soon forgotten. They stay with us. And although it's not a feeling we enjoy, pain serves a very important purpose. It shows us our errors and encourages us to release blocked emotional energy. It encourages us to *feel*, which is one of the principal advantages of having a body. And when we feel, we learn—and remember."

Chapter 20

"Come." He offered Karina his arm and lead her to the back of the cave. As they walked, the crystal grass crunched under their feet, calling to mind the way the ice had crunched during her first visit. "There's something I want to show you."

He led her toward a giant crystal, by far the largest in the cave, which sat on the ground toward the back. It was about five feet tall and resembled an egg sitting on its blunt end. It had a flat side facing them and was surrounded by dozens of glassy flowers.

As they approached, Karina realized that it occupied the same spot as the mirror that had shown her her past selves.

When they were a few feet away, a strange incandescent glow began to emanate from inside the crystal. Algernon positioned Karina in front of it, and the light began to pulse. She felt a tug on her like a magnet and noticed that it seemed to have an electrical charge.

When the hair on her arms stood up, she held out her forearm to show Algernon and giggled nervously.

After a moment, the light became solid and pictures began to form on the surface. He smiled and turned his attention toward the crystal.

"What do you see, Karina?" The image on the crystal's surface rippled like a reflection in a pond. As Karina watched, the image stabilized and a pretty lady in her thirties came into view. It was a scene in a park—or what looked like a park—where the lady was playing with a little girl and a fluffy, caramel-colored puppy. The little girl was still learning to walk and toddled around as they played a game of tag. The puppy sniffed the grass and wandered in circles nearby.

"It's a lady and her baby," said Karina. She felt a little silly describing a scene she knew he could see for himself. She opened her mouth to say that the lady and her baby were playing, but the sound never made it out.

Instead, she stood there mute, as it dawned on her that she knew this lady. As the lady smiled and played with her little girl, Karina studied her intently. Try as she might, though, she just couldn't place her. She searched the scene for clues to her identity but couldn't find any.

The adorable little girl, whose white dress was dotted with peach-colored daisies, was laughing hysterically while the lady looked on. Every gesture, every glance revealed her love for her daughter as well as her quiet confidence. Karina drew closer to the crystal and examined the lady's hair and clothes in an attempt to identify her.

Just then, the lady shifted, and Karina got a good look at her face. She jumped back, as if shocked by the crystal's electricity.

"Do you recognize her?" asked Algernon.

Unable to speak, Karina raised her hand and placed it over her chest. She looked to Algernon for confirmation, but all she got was an inscrutable grin.

She turned back to the crystal and gazed at the scene before her. Somewhere deep inside her, she knew she was being given a truly amazing gift: a glimpse of her future. And a very happy future it was.

"Is that my…?" Before she could finish, the little girl, who had taken to running in wobbly circles around the puppy, lost her footing. She toppled over and immediately began to wail, while the lady rushed to scoop her up. She hoisted the little girl into her lap and set about examining her knee.

The girl stopped crying long enough to peer down at the small cut. When she saw the tiny drop of blood forming there, she returned to sobbing and clutching at the lady's neck.

"Oh, dear!" said the lady, hugging her. "That looks terrible." Karina was stunned to hear own her voice coming from the lady's mouth. The lady took a tissue out of her pocket and dabbed at the cut. As she watched her mother working on her knee, the little girl sucked up her tears in an effort to be brave.

When the lady saw this, she gathered her daughter in her arms and stroked her back tenderly. The little girl gave into her tears and cried as her mother rocked her, while the puppy tried to nose its way between them.

"That's it, darling. Go ahead and cry if it hurts. It's okay." The girl wailed softly for a moment, her sobs flowing freely until they tapered off on their own. The lady held her close for a moment longer to make sure she was really done, then took her daughter's face in her hands and kissed it tenderly.

"There's no harm in tears, Sweetpea."

Inside the cave, Karina smiled when she heard this name and turned her attention to the little girl. There was something so enchanting about the way she moved and the light in her eyes that Karina was unable to take her eyes off her. Suddenly, she turned open-mouthed to Algernon.

"And the little girl?" he asked.

"It's… Grammy," said Karina quietly.

"Yes, Karina. She will come back to you."

Karina watched as the girl, now recovered, pushed away from her mother. After a moment, she was laughing and running around, a stray tear clinging to her cheek. The puppy resumed its playful chase.

"What else do you see?"

Karina was so engrossed by the incredible and yet completely mundane scene before her that she barely heard him. She concentrated on the details of the scene and saw the glow of happiness that would surround her as an adult. The lady's love for her child was like an orb of light encompassing them both.

Karina was just about to ask Algernon about the girl's father, when he entered the scene and gave them both a little squeeze. She felt she recognized his broad smile and the dimples under his eyes. For reasons she couldn't understand, he made her think of the sea.

She could feel her future husband's name beginning to form in her mind, when she noticed the expectant look on Algernon's face and realized that he was waiting for a response.

"She's in love." Karina's chest swelled with joy at the thought that she would one day live the life she saw before her.

"Yes. You will be happily married. You and your husband will build a joyful life together." A smile lit up Karina's face as Algernon took her by the arm and led her back toward the bridge.

"Many things in your life will change when you leave here tonight, Karina. You will notice it in many large and small ways. Know that everything is pointing you toward the future you have seen. You have accomplished a difficult task. You have healed yourself, which is the first step toward becoming the person you were always meant to be."

He turned and placed a hand on her shoulder.

"Your journey is not over. You must continue to bring the hidden pieces of yourself into the light."

Karina turned to go, glancing back for one last look at the crystal. Though she knew it was impossible, for a moment it seemed as if the lady had seen her here inside the cave. The undulating glow coming from the crystal made the lady's soft, contented smile appear to reach out toward her. I'm beautiful, thought Karina, placing a hand on her cheek.

Inside the crystal, the lady turned away to giggle at some inward joke.

Feeling a little like singing and a little like dancing, Karina was excited to see what would happen next. The huge grin on her face made Algernon smile, too.

He reached out his hand, but she was hesitant to take it, afraid that this handshake might mean their friendship was coming to an end. She was now quite certain she could live in expectation of a happy future. Still, she regretted having to say goodbye to her extraordinary friend.

"I'm proud of you, Karina. You're a brave young woman." Karina looked into his eyes, her smile tinged with sadness. He returned the gaze, his eyes brimming with pride and affection. They looked at each other for a long moment.

"Goodbye, my dear." He bowed gallantly and stretched out an arm to allow her to pass onto the bridge.

"Goodbye," Karina said, turning quickly to duck into the tunnel.

Before she knew it, she felt the slick river rocks beneath her feet. She emerged into the warm night air and the light of a full moon illuminating the creek bed. Remembering one last question she'd wanted to ask, she spun around and ran headlong into the dirt embankment. She reached up to finger the damp earth where the door had been only seconds before.

Caught between the "real" world and the subtle inner world, Karina stood there listening to the water trickling along the rocks. She breathed in the musty earth, and after a moment, turned to head back toward the trail.

A breeze had kicked up while Karina was inside the cave and now blew in gusts. As she made her way along the trail, the wind blew into her face, causing her hair and clothes to ripple around her.

Dust from the trail began to swirl and form dust devils, making it difficult to see. Seconds later, the wind was so strong it began to slow her progress along the trail. She stretched out her arms and allowed the wind to buffet them. The force of the gusts made it difficult to keep her eyes open.

With one especially strong blast, Karina felt almost as if she might lift off the ground. A curious buoyancy came to her feet, as if she were walking on air. And although startled by the unusual sensation, she kept her eyes pressed shut.

Then, in a momentary suspension of the laws of physics, her feet lifted off the ground. When the air blew back her legs like clothes on a clothes line, she was so startled, she couldn't help but open her eyes. She laughed nervously as she realized that she was hovering several feet above the ground, a human kite floating somewhere between shock and elation.

She began to climb, and the trail receded, while

her house, the neighbor boy's house, and part of the street came into view. But though she found herself high above the tree tops, Karina was not afraid of being blown away, because she could feel an invisible tether anchoring her to the ground.

Once again, she found herself wondering if what she was experiencing was a dream. She looked toward her house and saw her brothers through an upstairs window. They were sitting on the floor in front of the TV sharing a bowl of popcorn.

Another blast of wind hit her in the face, and she closed her eyes. When she opened them again, she was back on the ground. She dropped her arms, and the wind died down as quickly as it had blown up. She was left to ask herself what had just happened.

After a moment, she began walking and then ran the rest of the way up the trail. She bounded into the house, straight up the stairs, and burst into her brothers' room to find them exactly as she had seen them on the trail. They looked surprised by her sudden entrance.

"Want some popcorn, Karina?" asked Max. She chuckled in disbelief, shook her head, and closed the door behind her.

She went to her room and lay down on the bed. As she stared up at the ceiling, she imagined all the wonderful places her life might take her. The future she now knew awaited her made everything in the present—her dull, drab room; her often-annoying brothers; her boring, suburban town—seem infinitely more tolerable. She closed her eyes and, with her heart set on the future she'd seen in the cave, drifted off to sleep.

Epilogue

Twenty years have passed, and Karina has grown into the lady in the crystal vision. She smiles at her daughter in the foyer of their luxurious home.

"You ready?" she asks.

"Yeah!" says the little girl enthusiastically. The puppy barks and jumps in circles near the front door.

They climb into their SUV and drive to the park. Karina spreads a blanket on the grass, and they begin to play a game of tag. They feel the blood surging through their limbs and are gratefully, happily alive.

The little girl stumbles and falls. Karina stops to soothe her, speaking softly to her until she is up and running again. She turns to see her husband walking toward them from the parking lot. He crouches down to give them each a little hug.

She is about to stand up to resume the game, when she suddenly realizes where she is: playing in the park with her little girl. Today is the day she'd glimpsed in the cave all those years ago. It's the very moment she'd seen.

"And here I am!" she says quietly to herself. "It *was* real." Karina marvels at all that her life has become. For a moment, she stares into space and thinks about the sad, scarred girl she once was.

And laughs.

81290848R00113

Made in the USA
Columbia, SC
27 November 2017